Life, Liberty, and Property

Life, Liberty, and Property

The Economics and Politics of Land-Use Planning and Environmental Controls

Gordon C. Bjork
Claremont Men's College

LexingtonBooks
D.C. Heath and Company
Lexington, Massachusetts
Toronto

Library of Congress Cataloging in Publication Data

Bjork, Gordon C
   Life, liberty, and property.

   1. Land use—Planning—United States.   2. Land use—Environmental
aspects—United States.   3. Right of property—United States.   I. Title.
HD205.1980.B57   333.73′13′0973   80-8038
ISBN 0-669-03952-7

Second printing, January 1982

Published simultaneously in Canada

Printed in the United States of America

International Standard Book Number: 0-669-03952-7

Library of Congress Catalog Card Number: 80-8038

*To Susan,
who has always known
that land has values
apart from its price
and property has
responsibilities as well
as privileges*

Contents

Preface and Acknowledgments

The emotional origins of this book are to be found in Thoreau:

> We need the tonic of wilderness,
> to wade sometimes in marshes where
> the bittern and the meadow-hen lurk. . . .
> At the same time that we are earnest to
> explore and learn all things, we require
> that all things be mysterious and unexplorable. . . .
> We need to witness our own limits transgressed,
> and some life pasturing freely
> where we never wander.

The intellectual origins of this book are to be found in the economist's conceptual framework for evaluating choices. The economist's model takes note of the fact that in a world of increasing natural scarcity, the cost of preserving a little more of nature may be doing without some "civilization" and that choices between nature and civilization are inevitable, costly, and beneficial to some while harming or depriving others.

I began writing this book in 1975 as an ardent advocate of land-use planning and environmental legislation. I finished writing this book in 1979 as an opponent of environmental controls founded on the premise that progressively higher levels of government should tell individual citizens how they should behave in their management of land and the environment. I have not lost my personal desire to preserve and conserve the natural resources and natural beauty of our nation. I have found the root of most of our problems in our failure to define and protect individual and collective property rights to the use of the environment. Insofar as most land-use planning and environmental controls are directed to further attenuation of those rights or their redefinition to protect particular interest groups at the expense of others (usually the poor), I have come to expect that further governmental regulation of the environment is likely to exacerbate the problems of using natural resources in an efficient and equitable way.

I started this book with the conviction that economists could develop basic principles for the land-use planner or environmental regulator to attain greater efficiency in the use of the land and the environment. Alas, the notion of "efficiency" assumes a consensus about ends and the distribution of benefits. The notion that governmental planners could do things better than the voluntary arrangements between individuals for the exchange of use rights to the environment assumes that planners are maximizing the public's welfare rather than their own or the welfare of their political sponsors and allies.

While consideration of the problem of organizing the use of the environment gave me a new appreciation for the usefulness of private property rights, it also helped me understand that the efficiency and equity arguments for some of our existing legal arrangements were difficult to justify in a world of increasing resource scarcity and economic and personal interdependence. Thus the analysis in this volume will not accord with the preconceptions of either liberals or conservatives in its policy conclusions.

This book is written for diverse audiences whose common denominator is a concern for the environment. Primarily, it is addressed to the intelligent and concerned citizen. Secondarily, it is written for the economist who wants a better understanding of the historical and legal development of the property rights and conventions that presently control land use and the environment. It is also written for the lawyer or political scientist who wishes to gain an additional perspective on the interplay between economics, politics, and law in the control of the environment. Because it is written for diverse readers, the book has made inevitable compromises in content and style.

A few comments about structure: Chapter 1 examines the character of controversy over land-use planning and environmental controls in the context of the 1970s. It relates the controversies to the decision framework within which inevitable conflicts of interest must be resolved. Chapter 2 explores the elements of controversy over land-use planning: How serious are the "problems"? What has caused them? What can cure them? Chapter 2 also attempts to explain the contemporary character of policy debates in terms of long trends in resource scarcity and intellectual views about the natural world and social organization.

Property rights are the focus of chapter 3. Property rights to specific uses of specific resources are identified as means used by any society to make the economic choices of what goods and services shall be produced, how they shall be produced, and who shall enjoy them. The effects of particular configurations of property rights on a variety of resource-use patterns are explored. Contrasts are made between the feudal land-tenure rights of medieval Europe and modern freehold property rules to illustrate alternative ways of controlling land use. The role of property rights in internalizing some costs and benefits for the decision maker and externalizing others is seen to be the essential role of property-rights assignment in a society.

Chapter 4 investigates the ethical arguments that have been made by philosophers from Aristotle to Rawls to explain and justify particular kinds of property-rights configurations. The argument of the chapter emphasizes that it is very important to identify the sources of human action in the creation of property rights. Stability of possession, personal equation of costs and benefits, and avoidance of arbitrariness between citizens are recurrent themes in philosophical discussions of property rights.

The American legal framework for the resolution of conflicting claims to resource use is the subject of chapter 5. The particular focus of the discussion is the zoning issue and the limits placed on the zoning power.

Chapter 6 applies a neoclassical economic analysis to explain the price of land and the use of land. There is an elaboration of the theory to include expectations and taxes to explain the increase in the price of real estate relative to the prices of other capital assets and incomes in the 1970s. Chapter 7 investigates the probable effects of land-use planning on land prices, uses, and income distribution.

Chapter 8 attempts to tie together the preceding chapters to develop an analytical framework for evaluating alternative methods of controlling resource use. The discussion revolves around the criteria of equity, efficiency, and social objectives and attempts to summarize diverse considerations from historical, legal, economic, and philosophical insights for evaluation of land-use and environmental-control policies.

Chapter 9 is a program for change in existing American institutions and policies in five general areas: first, the treatment of air, water, and solitude as public property for which use fees must be paid when private use reduces the quantity or quality remaining for use by others; second, the strengthening of private rights to land use and the replacement of zoning with alternative methods of ensuring public health and safety; third, increased indicative land-use planning and governmental land purchases; fourth, substantial modification in existing income and property tax laws; and fifth, marginal cost pricing of public utility systems to new residential areas. Chapter 10 is a brief comment on the political realism of the recommended changes.

This book began as a study in the positive economics of land. It ended as a blend of positive and normative elements from economics, history, law, ethics, and politics. I hope it will be read and judged on those grounds. Most important, I hope it will have some positive effect in changing the real world as well as describing it.

Many individuals and several institutions have contributed to this book. In 1974-1975, I was both a visiting fellow of the Battelle Memorial Institute's Seattle Research Center and a visiting professor of economics at Oregon State University. Much of my initial reading and formulation of the problems took place during that period, and I would acknowledge a particular obligation to those institutions and to Dr. Ronald Paul of Battelle and Dean Emery Castle of OSU (now at Resources for the Future) for their support and encouragement.

Many colleagues, past and present, have made critical and constructive suggestions that have played a part in the development of my ideas. I would like to give specific thanks to Ross Eckert, Ward Elliott, Will Jones, Thomas Willett, and James Woodward, who read the manuscript in its entirety and offered a number of valid criticisms. My failure to adopt all the suggestions should absolve my colleagues from further responsibility for my unorthodox approach and conclusions. Finally, I would like to give due recognition to Sherry Couture and Ilene Campbell, whose intelligent transcription of manuscript into typescript played an important part in the production of this volume.

Life, Liberty, and Property

1 The Political Economy of Land-Use Planning and Environmental Controls

Ecology and economics were at the center of public policy concerns during the 1970s. The word *ecology* shares with *economics* a common (and commonplace) old root, *oikos,* the Greek word for "house." Ecology has been recently popularized as the study of the interdependence and interrelationship of all the physical and biological systems and processes on the earth. Most modern ecologists would be critical of the implication of human dominance semantically implied in the treatment of the world as "the household of man." Nevertheless, the study of ecology has assumed vital importance to the present and future human situation as man's activities have made an increasing impact on the world's physical and biological systems.

Aristotle coined, or at least popularized, the term *economics* to refer to the analysis of household activities concerned with providing food, clothing, and shelter. Most modern economists would chafe at the implied restriction of the scope of economics to household production and consumption of biological necessities. At least since the time of Karl Marx, they have understood the responsibilities of economic analysis for the explanation of social institutions as well as the analysis of the activities of production and consumption.

Ecology and economics have been increasingly juxtaposed as economic activity impacts ecological balance. Protection of the environment has become important because the suburbanization of America has threatened to destroy the environmental amenities that initially impelled people's relocation to the suburbs. Environmental activists may quote Emerson and Thoreau, but the responsive chord struck by their clarion calls has not been nineteenth-century romantic naturalism. It has been twentieth-century materialism, attempting to escape noise, traffic jams, dirty air, and polluted water. Environmental concern has become a major social concern because affluent Americans have suddenly discovered that they must *share* the environment with others. The public demands for land-use planning, resource conservation, and environmental protection have occurred because the American people have had to solve the problems of diminishing living space and diminishing returns.

Diminishing returns, the Ricardian analysis of the Malthusian assertion that population must inevitably press upon the earth's limited resources, has become an important world reality contemporaneously with the growth of

1

environmental concern in the United States. World catches of fish trebled between 1950 and 1970 and subsequently declined, despite increasing effort, because of the partial exhaustion of biological stocks. Food prices have risen relative to other prices in the 1970s as food production, worldwide, has failed to keep pace with the demands of a growing population.

The tenfold increase in energy prices during the 1970s has been popularly ascribed to the greed of the Organization of Petroleum Exporting Countries (OPEC), oil companies, and the failure of U.S. government policies. A more realistic long-run explanation would call attention to the pricing of energy in terms of the rapidly rising replacement costs of fuels with higher and higher recovery costs in the future.[1]

The process of social change is dimly understood by those who live through it. The sixteenth-century Italians who were parties to the Renaissance did not understand the implications of the rediscovery of classical knowledge for their social and political institutions. The nineteenth-century Britons who transformed their modes of production and transportation were only vaguely aware that they were taking part in the Industrial Revolution that would transform their social institutions as well as their modes of production.

The people of the United States are experiencing a period of rapid change that destabilizes existing social institutions and necessitates the reexamination and restructuring of legal, economic, and political organization. Unfortunately, the rapidity of change has led to overreaction in attitudes and actions. Stunned by the putrefaction of Lake Erie or phase-III smog alerts, many Americans have transformed their conception of the natural environment from a dumping ground to an object of religious devotion. The reaction to previous profligacy has been a conversion to fanatical devotion to environmental protection.[2]

From New England to California, from Florida to the Pacific Northwest, recent years have witnessed conflict and controversy over the control and use of the environment. American concern with environmental quality has intensified as the American dream of a house and garden and material affluence has been diminished by increases in the price of food and housing relative to disposable incomes.

The building of a nuclear power station on the New Hampshire coast has been delayed interminably by controversy over the effects on marine life of the hot-water discharge. Meanwhile, the economy of New England and the standard of living of its residents continues to decline in the face of rapidly rising prices of imported oil.

In California the Coastline Commission has severely limited the development of land proximate to the coast, and continual battles are waged by various sectional groups over the control of water. Housing prices in southern California *trebled* during the seven years from 1971 to 1978. The cost of free-flowing rivers in the Sierra for white-water enthusiasts has been increased food prices for the rest of the nation.

Environmental groups in Washington, Oregon, and California have pressured the Forest Service and the Bureau of Land Management to limit the harvesting of timber. Lumber prices trebled between 1970 and 1980. The northwest states have been in dispute among themselves about the allocation of the Columbia's waters and the electricity generated by them. The awareness increases that water is a limited resource needing careful management.

In Florida the development of swampland has wrought great changes in the water table, threatening agriculture and urban water supplies, while in Tennessee the protection of a rare species of fish, the tiny snail darter, has interrupted the completion of a multimillion dollar dam that would lessen dependence on fossil fuels for electricity generation and protect land from flooding.

In the Rockies, people are asking why Wyoming should be strip-mined to air-condition Chicago. The Indians of the Four Corners area of New Mexico ask why their air should be polluted to lessen the pollution from coal-fired power stations in southern California.

All over the United States there are controversies about the siting of freeways, factories, and shopping centers. The farms and forests near urban areas are converted to suburb or allowed to decay in anticipation of their development. And, in most of the United States, the price of land and houses has been increasing much faster than disposable incomes, forcing American families to devote a larger part of their incomes to the purchase of less and less space.

Concern over the availability and distribution of land and environmental amenity has led many Americans to ask whether the economic, social, and legal framework for the control of land, water, and the ambient air is adequate in view of increasing population and technological change that is land consumptive. There have been widespread statements about the need for increased governmental intervention in the control of land use.

In addition to federal and state legislation to increase environmental protection, the early 1970s brought a great increase in legislative activity in the United States in land-use planning. Bills were narrowly defeated in several congressional sessions to require (or offer substantial inducements and penalties to) individual states to adopt statewide land-use plans. Six states (Hawaii, Oregon, Vermont, Montana, Colorado, and Florida) passed various forms of legislation providing for state land-use plans and regulations.

Once passed and operative, there were reactions against land-use planning in every state where bills were passed. Montana's was repealed, and in every state there has been substantial disillusionment with land-use planning on the part of both proponents and opponents.

Part of the disillusionment can be explained by conflicts of interest and the windfall gains and losses that occurred from initial attempts at land-use planning. Part of it can be explained by bureaucratic delay and confusion.

I submit, however, that much of the disillusion occurred because the problems were much more complex than the planners realized.

Land-use planning is a vague and comprehensive term that serves as an umbrella for a variety of different programs and approaches designed to shift the control of land from the individual owner to higher levels of governmental authority. Land-use planning can be considered at several levels of analysis. It might be viewed as another aspect of the continuing attempt to shift the locus of responsibility for decisions affecting land use from lower to higher levels of government to achieve better coordination. Or it might be viewed as further elaboration of traditional governmental responsibility for zoning, or provision of public services such as streets, sewers, parks, and schools. Or it might be viewed as part of a fundamental modification of the relationships between individuals and the state in the locus of responsibility for land-use control.

This book will consider land-use planning from several aspects and at several levels. A fundamental objective of the analysis, however, is to indicate that the arguments for land-use planning are premised on the assumption that the state can and *should* redefine and reallocate property rights in land and not merely enforce the property rights that happen to have come about from the choices and transactions of individual members of society.

This assumption about the role of government involves a rejection of one of the basic premises of our social, economic, political system — the premise that every individual should have the right to pursue his own interests, within the limits set by law, without regard for the interests of others *because* this will lead to the greatest social welfare. And it involves the acceptance of the premise that the state can redistribute and redefine property rights in such a way that society can be "better off" as a result.

The fundamental objective of the proponents of land-use planning in the United States is to shift the control of land and other natural resources from individuals and lower levels of government to higher levels of government. There are two basic arguments for doing this; one is the greater efficiency of more centralized planning. The other is the equity, or distributional, argument that individuals or local governments may be unable or unwilling to undertake some types of decisions about land use because those decisions would be detrimental to their interests or to those of their constituents.

What's wrong, according to the critics, with our present use of land and natural resources? Why is sweeping change seen to be necessary? The first aspect of the problem is waste. It is alleged that we are cutting down forests, pumping oil, mining groundwater, overfishing the oceans, paving over farmland, and destroying the natural fertility of the soil. One aspect of the criticism is the intertemporal allocation of resources. If we cut forests now, we will not have them next year (although we might have them seven or eight decades hence). Farmland paved over now may be lost to future generations except at prohibitively high costs of reclamation.

Another aspect of the waste problem is inefficiency. Urban sprawl, for example, is said to be an "inefficient" use of land, labor, capital, and energy. Sprawling subdivisions require more space and capital for roads, and the automobiles they necessitate take more labor, capital, and energy in their construction and operation than would rapid-transit systems. Sprawling subdivisions require more capital investment in public utility collection and distribution systems for water, sewer, garbage, gas, electricity, and school transportation.

A second category of problems cited by critics of existing institutions for the control of land use is the adverse effects of some land uses on other people. Excessive noise and pollution of air and water, are prime examples. The use of the automobile, necessitated by urban sprawl, is one large generator of air pollution. Agriculture and forestry practices that change the seasonal variations in stream flow through the destruction of watersheds are another example. The noise effects of factories are one example. In all these cases, it is argued that existing institutional arrangements make it difficult for landowners and users to take into account either the beneficial or deleterious effects of their actions on others.

A third category of problems created by contemporary land-use patterns and institutions is the preservation of natural areas, areas of great scenic beauty, recreational value, or areas of cultural or historical interest. What happens to the public's enjoyment of Sunday walks or drives through farmland when the farmland is turned into subdivisions? What happens to the public's enjoyment of forests when they are logged? Or seacoasts when they are developed? What happens to our understanding of the past when historic buildings are turned into amusement parks? What role does free access to certain scenic or historic places have in our priorities? Or our rights as citizens?

A fourth category of problems cited in connection with contemporary economic institutions' controlling land use is income distribution. Why should the owners of oil wells or water rights receive large incomes from exploitation of resources that were naturally created? Why should income be redistributed from suburban homeowners to speculators, or the former owners of land, or to developers in the process of land conversion? Scarcity rather than work creates those "economic rents." What role does unequal ownership of land play in the inequality of income and wealth in contemporary America?

The opponents of change in our present practices of administering land and natural resources have ready answers to the alleged problems. They do not concede that the problems are serious. They do not admit that they cannot be handled by present institutional mechanisms. They allege that the restriction or abandonment of private property, or change in the present dispersion of powers for decisions respecting land and resource use among a variety of governmental levels and agencies, would be subversive of individual freedom and conducive to arbitrary and authoritarian control of the individual by the state.

Individual landowners are not the only people opposing, or having reservations about, more centralization of land-use planning. Governments are not monolithic. Various agencies of the federal government have conflicting interests in the shaping of national legislation that would affect the control of land by such federal agencies as the Bureau of Land Management, the Forest Service, the Corps of Engineers, and the Defense Department.

County governments have been the chief lobbyists against state land-use plans both before Congress and state legislatures because they do not wish to lose power to state agencies in the control of land use. In at least one state (Oregon) where a law providing for land-use planning has been passed, the legislative compromises necessary for getting the state involved in land-use planning left county governments responsible for drawing up land-use plans consistent with state land-use objectives. This compromise preserved a great deal of local authority and autonomy in the planning process for county governments. Some would argue that it vitiates the effectiveness of comprehensive planning.

To attempt to limit the powers of local governments to escape or modify the provisions of the statewide plan, the Oregon Supreme Court has held (*Baker* v. *City of Milwaukee*) that once the county plan has been established, variances may not be granted except by modification of the county plan itself on demonstration that the variance requested is in keeping with the objectives of the state plan.

The objective of land-use planners is to centralize control of land-use decisions. The arguments for land-use planning by higher levels of government emphasize the need for coordination and allocation at higher levels of governmental responsibility. Their real intent and effect is to change the locus of decisions about who will pay and who will benefit.

The decision of a developer to build a thousand homes on an erstwhile farm may involve the neighboring community in large incremental costs for water, schools, sewer treatment, and police and fire services, and depress property values in existing neighborhoods.

The decision of a coastal county to zone for vacation-home subdivisions may deprive other citizens of easy access to the ocean for recreation at the same time that it raises property values and lowers tax rates for the landowners of the county.

The decision of a county adjacent to a city to zone large-lot subdivisions may create the need for an extensive system of state highways and freeways and substantially increase air pollution.

The decision of a municipality to site an airport in a certain location may fundamentally change the character of an adjoining area, necessitating large public expenditures for roads and utilities, and exposing nearby residents to high levels of noise that destroy part of their enjoyment of their homes.

The decision to locate a prison in an area may have adverse effects on local residents. The decision of the Navy, or the Corps of Engineers, or the Atomic Energy Commission, to site a facility may have a variety of wanted and unwanted effects.

Every land-use decision creates winners and losers by its effects on land values, taxes, and environmental amenities. Who should decide the land uses that create gains and losses? Individual owners? Counties? Cities? States? Agencies of the federal government? Costs and benefits are inevitable. Who shall decide to whom they accrue?

A major thrust of this book is to explore the inevitability of choices based on conflicts of interest. The proponents of land-use planning often ignore the distributional character of land-use decisions by treating land-use questions primarily as *efficiency* questions. They ask, "If America has a limited amount of land and other natural resources, how should their use be organized to meet our social objectives?" However, that question presumes that land scarcity is a serious problem, that we presently lack procedures to organize land use effectively, and that we possess, as a society, well-defined objectives that could be better realized by some different set of institutions or decision makers.

Because the questions and arguments raised about land-use planning by its proponents and opponents frequently beg the presumptions about scarcity, about procedures and institutions, and about social objectives, they begin from the wrong point. The question is not whether land is scarce, but rather what is the extent and nature of the scarcity; the question is not whether we should have land-use planning but rather what kind of land-use planning mechanisms we should have; the question is not whether there should be public control over the private use of land but what kinds of land-use control should be exercised by which public agencies for what purposes. The most fundamental questions in land-use planning are about who should benefit from land-use decisions and who should lose. They are questions about equity.

There is, currently functioning, a very complex set of rules, administered by all levels of government, that controls land use. Anyone who has attempted to develop or change the use of land is aware of their scope and complexity. It has been estimated that the cost of delays and additional administrative expense for complying with present rules adds 20 percent to the cost of a new home. The problem is not the absence of rules. Apart from the overlapping and contradictory land-use policies followed by various levels of governments, there is no social consensus about how land *should* be used. This is the source of the problem. This is why there is continuing controversy over zoning, the siting of dams, power plants, and roads, and extensive criticism of land-use plans at every level of government.

Land used for a housing development cannot be used for a farm. Building an oil refinery on a salt marsh will remove a natural area from public use. At the most basic level, if one person uses land for his own purposes, it precludes another from using it for his. This is the nature of scarcity and the scarcity of nature. This is the source of the conflict that leads to the creation of institutions to allocate and distribute land and other resources.

The problem we face in land-use control institutions is not the lack of a set of rules or "bad" social institutions to control land use but conflicts of interest between individuals. The problem to be solved is the reconciliation of those inevitable conflicts of interest.

Reconciliation of the conflict of interests has always been accomplished by the social definition of property rights — by the specification of which individuals have rights to do specific things with resources. The social cost of using any resource is the opportunity foregone of alternative uses.

The establishment of clearly defined and transferable property rights to the use of resources is *the* important element in the reconciliation of conflicts of interest. The logic of granting property rights to the use of a parcel of land to one individual is that he then has a strong incentive to use it for its most highly valued use or to transfer it by sale or exchange to someone else who will. This is the logic of our private property system. Conflicts over use arise when property rights are ill-defined or in dispute. When this occurs, the results may be inefficient and/or inequitable.

Both the legal and economics professions have contributed to confusions in this area by regarding certain uses of resources as "nuisances" or "externalities" or "spillover" effects. Thus, to cite a classic and hackneyed example, the factory owner who allowed his smoking chimney to blacken his neighbor's laundry would be held by the lawyer to be committing a "nuisance" and by the economist to be imposing an "external cost" or "spillover effect." The critical point to remember in an interdependent world is that a nuisance to one party is a valuable property right to another.

The social cost of using any resource is the opportunity foregone or the cost imposed on other social activities. Using the air to carry away wastes rather than controlling emissions lessens the cost of production. But it also increases the costs of keeping houses and clothes clean. The environment, like any natural resource, has a variety of uses. All have social costs.

The first jurist (to my knowledge) to articulate this point clearly was Justice Brandeis in his dissenting opinion in the *Pennsylvania Coal* v. *Mahon* case (cited extensively in chapter 4). In this case, Brandeis argued that the law ought to make the coal-mine owner explicitly take into account the reduction in the value of surface land caused by the subsidence that was the consequence of certain mining practices.

The first economist to deal comprehensively with this problem was R.H. Coase in a seminal article, "The Problem of Social Cost."[3] In this article, Coase developed the principle that if property rights to resource use were clearly defined and transferable, and if there were no transactions costs or imperfect knowledge to distort the bargaining powers of the parties in conflict over resource use, the assignment of property rights to one party or the other would not affect the use of the resource over which there was conflict — only the distribution of gains from its use.

A definitive working principle for the allocation of property rights in the face of conflicts has been developed by Joseph Sax in "Taking, Private Property, and Public Rights."[4] Elaborating the principles put forward by Brandeis and Coase, Sax posited that property rights should be specified and allocated to make the burdened party in any conflict the party most capable financially, organizationally, and technologically, of dealing with the problem. Thus the airline that creates noise or the pulp mill that discharges wastes should be made liable for the costs imposed on others by their productive activities (with the costs ultimately borne by the consumers of the products or services made possible by those activities that alter the environment). The burden of liability should be placed with the proximate source of resource use because of the organizational and technological advantages that would most likely lend to the most efficient management of the resource.

My analysis draws heavily on Brandeis, Coase, and Sax as it explains social institutions as an attempt to maximize social output and minimize social conflict, by defining property rights in ways that will be efficient and equitable. Land-use planning, and environmental controls, are evaluated as part of man's continuing efforts to resolve conflicts of interest in a world of both increasing scarcity and increasing interdependence.

Notes

1. For an elegant exposition of the rational theory of pricing exhaustible resources, see R. Solow, "The Economics of Resources or the Resources of Economics," *American Economic Review* 64, (no. 2) (May 1974).

2. Kenneth Boulding observes that the concept of a natural equilibrium or a stable ecosystem is a myth. Physical and biological relationships are in constant change and flux. There is no biological reason to view one organism as more "natural" than another or any physical rationale to view a rock as more "natural" than a rusting car body. Distinctions about what is "natural" or "part of the ecosystem" rest on normative judgments. It is impossible to separate man and his artifacts from the "natural" environment. The personification of nature is just a romantic substitute for religious faith to serve as a basis for values. For a more extensive discussion, see Kenneth

Boulding, *Ecodynamics: A New Theory of Societal Evolution* (Beverly Hills, Calif.: Sage Publications, 1978).

3. R.H. Coase, "The Problem of Social Cost," *Journal of Law and Economics* 3 (October 1960).

4. Joseph L. Sax, "Taking, Private Property and Public Rights," *Yale Law Journal* 81 (no. 2) (December 1971).

The Issues in
Resource-Use Conflicts

The controversy over land-use planning has a number of elements. The first is differences of definition and measurement of the extent of land scarcity. The second is disagreement over the way in which present institutions governing land use, particularly private property, work. The third is differing value judgments about the relative importance of land-related goods and services — food, energy, living space, aesthetic environmental amenitities — and who should enjoy them.

It is important to keep these elements of controversy in focus because it is differences in judgments and opinions about the state of affairs in the physical and economic world, about the effects of social institutions, and about values that lead to disagreement about the nature of the problems of land-use control.

It is important to realize that the problems of land use are relative both to the technologies, and resource bases of the physical world, and to the values and expectations of a society. "Problems" do not exist in the world. They are intellectual constructs. Problems are identified by people whose perception of how the world *is* differs from their expectations of how the world *ought* to be. Suburban sprawl is not considered to be a problem to people who enjoy suburban life. To them it is a "solution" rather than a "problem."

This may seem an elementary distinction, but it is necessary to make it at the outset because human beings must always make choices about the way in which they deal with scarcity as they organize their economic and social activity. These choices involve expectations about the resulting patterns of activity and value judgments about the social desirability of different states of affairs.

The Extent of Scarcity

Let us consider, for illustrative purposes, some of the current arguments for land-use planning. Urban deterioration and suburban sprawl have been going on for centuries, but modern transportation technologies — particularly the private automobile — have greatly increased the pace and extent of the "problem" in the United States. Consider conflicting statements on the extent of the phenomenon. Senator Henry Jackson, in introducing the Land Resource Planning Assistance Act in 1975, said,

11

Over the next thirty years, an additional 19.7 million acres of undeveloped land will be consumed by urban sprawl — an area equivalent to the states of New Hampshire, Vermont, Massachusetts, and Rhode Island.

Each decade's new growth will absorb an area greater than the entire state of New Jersey.

Each year the equivalent of 2½ times the Oakland-San Francisco metropolitan region must be built to meet the Nation's housing goals.

By the year 2000, over 3.5 million acres may be paved over for highways and airports.

By the end of the century, five million acres of valuable agricultural land may be lost to public facilities, second home development and waste control projects, and another seven million may be taken for recreation areas.

Finally, in the next two decades, one industry alone — the energy industry — will require vast areas of land; new high voltage transmission lines will consume 3 million acres of new rights of way while nearly four hundred new major generating stations will require hundreds of thousands of acres of prime industrial sites.[1]

On the other hand, a well-known economist wrote in a government-sponsored volume devoted to the question of resource adequacy:

Compared to most developed countries of the world, these figures (on land per capita) are very large. In 1967, the United States had a population of 55 persons per square mile. The corresponding figure for France was 237; for West Germany, 624; for the United Kingdom, 588; and for Europe as a whole, 239. Even when one takes account of differences in terrain, fertility of the soil, and international trade, these are dramatic differences.

But what about the future. Are we destined to live at densities comparable to those experienced in Europe? Are we paving over large amounts of good agricultural and recreational land? Thirty years from now, will we still have sufficient agricultural and recreational land to maintain an economy and way of life comparable to what we know today?

One way to shed some light on these questions is to make fairly generous assumptions about future land requirements and compare them with aggregate supplies of land. Suppose, for example, we assume that land associated with human habitation, business, and transportation expands more or less in proportion to the increase in population. Suppose, moreover, we take estimates of future recreational land requirements from Chapter 6 an outdoor recreation, and hold this per capital figure constant as we vary population assumptions for the year 2000. For future agricultural land requirements, we can use the estimates presented in Chapter 7 on the agricultural sector, assuming first, that there is no restriction on the use of chemical fertilizers and pesticides and, that there is such a restriction so that additional land must be used to obtain the output. . .

The first and most obvious result is that, even under the high population growth assumption, the United States will still be classified as a relatively land-rich country. Per capita acres would drop from 11 to 7 by the year 2000; but even this latter figure is higher than what most European countries have at their disposal today. On the other hand, compared to what Americans are accustomed; this is a sizeable irreversible reduction that will require some adjustments.

Second, we do not appear to be "paving over" large quantities of land, at least not in the aggregate. Land devoted to human habitation, transport, industry, ports, etc.—which includes urban parks and many other areas that are not covered by man-made structures—increased from 2.9 percent in 1970 to somewhere between 3.9 percent and 4.7 percent (of the total land area of the United States under different population growth assumptions). Of course, within specific geographic areas, a much higher percentage of the land may become covered. But in the aggregate, the change between 1970 and 2000 does not seem very dramatic."[2]

There are substantial differences of opinion among informed observers as to the extent and seriousness of resource scarcity.

The source of the "problem" cited by advocates of land-use planning is scarcity. Zoning land for open space is only important if land is so scarce, relative to the demand for it, that open spaces will disappear. Mandating more or less intensive use of land than would result from market decisions is only necessary if it is believed that the market will not deal adequately with present or future scarcity.

Scarcity is a basic fact of human existence. All societies, from time immemorial, have created rules and institutions to deal with scarcity. The study of political economy, which examines the way in which men organize institutions to allocate scarce resources among the competing demands of the members of a society distinguishes three main types of structures for decision making: tradition, the market, and centralized allocation. The United States has primarily utilized the market for land-use allocation for the last two centuries. How extensively do market operations need to be modified to achieve satisfactory results in land allocation? Or is centralized allocation inevitable?

Land has not always been a scarce resource for the people of the United States. We have already noted that there is a difference of opinion about how scarce land is now or will be in the future. Economists say that a resource is scarce if there is a demand for it at a zero price. There is land in the Nevada desert or the Alaskan tundra that presently commands only a nominal price. There is some urban slum real estate that has such limited income potential relative to its tax and building code liabilities that its owners have abandoned it. Nevertheless, most land in the United States presently commands a positive price, and the price of many kinds of land has been rising faster than the general price level during the past several decades.[3]

The people of the United States occupy a finite land mass in a finite world. The U.S. population is increasing. The population of the world is growing. The ratio of people to land and natural resources is increasing.

The ratio of population to resources and the rate of growth of population relative to capital and land-saving technology are important determinants of social institutions and the level and character of economic activity.[4]

The Effects of Institutions

Increasing population pressure and land scarcity do not necessarily need the modification or abandonment of private property or "the market" as a means of controlling land use. In historical fact, transferable property rights in land were the institutional solution to increasing land scarcity at the end of the medieval period in Europe. Private property in land, and the development of markets for its sale or rental, accompanied the increasing scarcity of land relative to labor and capital in medieval Europe. It can be argued (see chapter 3) that the problems connected with increasing scarcity of land relative to labor and capital could be solved by *more* extensive use of the market and removal of institutional barriers to its efficient operation.

Opinions differ about the effectiveness of social institutions in dealing with land use during a period of increasing scarcity. Consider again Senator Jackson's comments in introduction of the Land Resource Planning and Assistance Act:

> It has become increasingly obvious to environmentalists and industrialists alike, to both urban and rural interests, and to private citizens and public officials that the problem of exponential growth in the last quarter of the 20th century cannot be met with 19th century laws and procedures. We simply cannot afford to continue to absorb the enormous costs in economics losses, delays, resource misallocations, and adverse social and environmental effects which have been and will be exacted by our failure to plan for the sound and balanced use of our land base. In the past, many land resource decisions were the exclusive province of those whose interests were selfish, short term, and private. In the future—in the face of immense pressures on our limited land resource—these decisions must be long-term and public.[5]

The need for new procedures for land-use control have not been "obvious" enough to pass legislation!

It is difficult to find a single quote that adequately defends the elements of the present system—private property, local zoning, state and local control over the spatial distribution of economic activity. An argument for the present system, however, would point to the material welfare and relative freedom from governmental regulations of the bulk of the U.S. population in comparison with the populations of other countries. An important argument for the strengths and weaknesses of the present system of land-use control would be an analysis of alternative mechanisms for making allocational decisions. As one bumper sticker aptly expressed it, "If you like the U.S. Postal Service, you'll love federal land-use planning."

The Impact of Values

The third element of controversy about the effectiveness of present institutions for land-use control involves judgments about human values and equity. To use the example of suburbanization, who has gained and who has lost from the land-use trends of the recent past? We have increasing air pollution from the use of the private automobile and the diffusion of the population that has required us to become an automobile-centered culture. On the other hand, there is the opportunity for families to enjoy suburban gardens rather than the tenements of a half-century ago. Suburban sprawl is identified as a reason for land-use planning on the grounds that it creates "problems" that need to be solved. But the attribution of a problem to the phenomena we subsume under the term "suburbanization" involves generalizations about the situation in the physical world, attribution of causation to existing institutional mechanisms, and value judgments about the results. In other words, what some people view as a serious problem, others see as a good solution.

The Dynamics of Change

The current groundswell of concern for new approaches to land-use controls arises from three changes that have been taking place in our society — population-land ratios, land-consumptive technologies, and changes in cultural values. These have led to demands for change in institutional mechanisms for land-use control.

American social and political institutions were developed at a time when land was abundant and the people and capital to develop the land were scarce. Consequently, the land-use policies of the past were aimed at settlement and development. The opportunity to own land was the inducement that drew many immigrants from Europe. Free or cheap land was the driving force behind westward expansion across the continent. Large blocks of land were given or sold at nominal prices to individuals, corporations, or states by the British Sovereign before Independence and the federal government thereafter. Small blocks of land were granted free to individuals under the Homestead Act (1862) in return for their settlement and development. Mineral claims can still be patented on federal lands. But land is no longer cheap and its market price is rising.

The objectives of land-use policies in the past were simple. The people of the United States were interested in promoting the growth of population and growth of economic activity. The granting of private, freehold property rights in land and natural resources provided inducements for immigration, western expansion, and the investment of labor and capital in land and resources to make them productive.

The objectives of the United States in population growth and resource development are no longer shared by all. We have restricted immigration. There is great popular interest in limiting the growth of the population through lowering birth rates. The "zero-population growth" ethic has its economic counterpart in the "steady-state" economy. There is substantial public sentiment for the preservation of open spaces and the limitation of further land development.

About one third of the nation's surface area remains in governmental ownership, but most of that land is more suitable for extensive grazing, forestry, or recreation than for development. The remaining two thirds of the nation's land is in private (including corporate) ownership. Should the private control of land be further restricted and controlled? Does private ownership of land lead to exploitation or conservation? What is exploitation or conservation? Is exploitation bad and conservation good?

The changes in our situation—population-land ratios, land-consumptive technologies, changes in cultural values—are real. They are the facts of our contemporary situation. Our institutions were developed in a different historical situation. The form of social institutions, of property conventions, tax laws, regulations, and administrative procedures must agree with the functions a society expects them to perform. They must also be appropriate to the technology that a society employs in using land, water, and air.

I believe that we are in the middle of a fundamental change, "a quiet revolution,"[6] in American attitudes toward the use of land and other natural resources. The change is a shift in emphasis from development to conservation. One source of the attitudinal change is a recognition of limits to growth and development. Another aspect of the change has been the affirmation of man's need for nature *and* man's need for satisfactory human relationships as well as material goods and economic security.[7] A third aspect of the change is a greater interest in equality of shares in contemporary affluence.

The change in the attitudes toward land and resource use is part of a larger conceptual change in the way in which man views the world. The change has several facets. One facet is the recognition of the interdependence of physical and biological systems, the recognition that our universe is a complex ecosystem in which every part affects some other part. Another facet is the recognition that man's economic activities take place within this self-contained ecosystem and have far-reaching interdependencies. A third facet is the recognition that *homo sapiens,* alone among the residents of the ecosystem, has some potential capacity to control his own destiny and that of the ecosystem itself by the rules and institutions he establishes to control his behavior.

It is tempting to compare the changes in the conceptual framework for analyzing human institutions that are taking place in our decade with those that have occurred in earlier periods of human history in response to such thinkers as Newton or Darwin. Newton's conception of the universe as a giant equilibrium system caused philosophers such as John Locke, Adam Smith, and Thomas Jefferson to think that there were natural laws that controlled human behavior. From this premise they inferred that it was the role of social, economic, and political institutions to see that these laws could work smoothly to produce the natural justice of equilibrium outcomes from the operation of these forces. The state did not have a positive role other than ensuring that these forces could work with a minimum of friction.

Darwin's views on the process of evolution by natural selection, on the other hand, caused analysis and evaluation of social institutions to emphasize the functionalist and relativist characteristics of those institutions, but the institutions were not to interfere with the "survival of the fittest." Darwin's theories, like Newton's, were used to justify a noninterventionist state. "Social Darwinism" was an enormously influential determinant of social organization in the United States between the end of the Civil War and World War II.

The analysis of social and political institutions in our time has been powerfully affected by nondeterminist, disequilibrium models of the natural world. Einstein and Heisenberg have overthrown Newtonian physics. In fact, Keynes's rejection of the self-equilibrating stability of macroeconomic forces could be considered a sequel. In biology, the work of Crick and Watson in genetics has opened up a whole new field of research and experimentation with investigation into replacing "natural selection" with "genetic engineering." Contemporaneously, writers such as Rachel Carson, Barry Commoner, and Paul Ehrlich have tried to warn their readers that the impact of human technology on the biological world is leading to disastrous consequences for future generations.[8]

Conceptual changes in scientific analysis in the physical and biological sciences have led many social scientists and social activists to call for massive changes in social institutions and, in particular, to advocate central planning to avoid the negative consequences of individual exploitation of the physical and biological universe. There has been increasing skepticism about the capability of private property and the market system to produce acceptable results in the use of land, water, air, natural resources, and the environment.

. This book is not concerned with the history of ideas. It is rather an examination of the contemporary American institutions utilized to control the use of land and other natural resources. Yet it cannot be emphasized too strongly at the outset that practical questions — such as whether zoning should be implemented at the county or state level, or whether pollution costs should be borne by all users of air and water or be imposed on those who contaminate the ecosystem with harmful effluents — depend crucially on fundamental assumptions about the limits placed by the ecosystem on the form and extent of economic activity. They also depend on beliefs about the appropriate relationships between persons, and between individuals and the state, and men's beliefs about their responsibilities for the welfare of others in the present and future generations.

The restructuring of social institutions — particularly basic institutions like property rights, individual rights, and taxation — always occurs in response to particular situations that present problems or opportunities to the members of that society. If an enemy attacks, citizens are drafted to resist the aggression. If fertile land is available and there is a need for more food, property rights are assigned to guide individuals to exploit the opportunity. If one subgroup in the society feels its interests are poorly served by existing institutions and practices, it seeks to expand its opportunities relative to the freedom of other groups to treat with the disadvantaged group in particular ways. If air pollution imposes costs, attempts will be made to shift those costs.

While institutions are structured by responses to particular problems, they inevitably change the relationship between citizens and the state as they change the relationship between citizens. When members of a society call upon government to change the relationship between citizens, they inevitably yield the power to the state to define those relationships in the future rather than merely enforcing the voluntary relationships worked out by citizens among themselves. Concern that the state should not interfere in the accommodation of conflicts among individuals is a prime concern of many opponents of more centralization of land-use power.

Biases and Conclusions

Some modification of our institutions controlling land use is needed. The decisions made by individuals (and corporations) about land use do not always result in allocative efficiency. The transactions costs and uncertainties inherent in our present organization of land use are too great. Property rights and zoning practices need to be redefined and reallocated to conserve and use our natural resources more efficiently.

More action is needed at the local and state level to ensure access by the population to areas of scenic beauty and historic interest. The provision of these public goods should be recognized as a public decision with real costs, and those costs should be borne by the public and not avoided by uncompensated arbitrary restrictions on the use of property by present owners.

The distribution of income needs to be recognized as resulting both from social decisions about the definition of property rights and from historical accidents. Some of the inequality that results from the unequal ownership of scarce natural assets should be redistributed to accord with contemporary beliefs about distributive justice and to bind all members of our society in support of our social institutions.

Having stated some of my conclusions, let me also state my conviction that private property is the fundamental basis of our economic, political, and social systems. Its definition and distribution can be modified, as in the past, but great care must be exercised to avoid actions by government that are arbitrary *as between citizens* and that lack a reciprocity of advantage for all.

I do *not* believe that the practice of land-use planning ought to be regarded as an extension of the practice of zoning in providing environmental amenity. Individual decisions operating with existing institutions are unable to provide that amenity on as extensive a basis as desired. It should be understood that zoning is not a way of providing public goods at private expense.[9]

Private property in land, freehold ownership, came about in various European countries some centuries ago because bilateral or multilateral arrangements among individuals could not provide the incentives necessary to individuals to use and develop land in a socially beneficial manner. Zoning restrictions came into general use in the United States a century ago for the same reason. I believe the time has come to further modify the socially contrived arrangements for the regulation of land use to deal more adequately with the new problems created by income and population growth, technological change, and changing human values. But before we modify those arrangements, a clear understanding of their logic and development is important.

Notes

1. U.S., Congress, Senate, *Congressional Record,* 94th Cong., 1st sess., 1975, 121:36, p. 3205.

2. Ronald Ridker, "Future Water Needs and Supplies with a Note on Land Use," in *Population, Resources, and the Environment,* ed. R. Ridker, U.S. Commission on Population Growth and the American Future (Wash-

ington, D.C.: Government Printing Office, 1972), pp. 222-227.

3. Between 1970 and 1980, the value of farm real estate trebled while the general price level doubled. *Economic Report of the President January 1980* (Washington, D.C.: Government Printing Office, 1980), tables B-49 and B-95.

4. One recent book on the process of economic growth has argued that the increase of population relative to available arable land was the primary determinant of the breakdown of feudal tenure and the medieval open-field system and its replacement with private property rights to land. See Douglas North and Robert Thomas, *The Rise of the Western World: A New Economic History* (Cambridge, United Kingdom: Cambridge University Press, 1973).

5. *Congressional Record* p. 3205.

6. The term "quiet revolution" comes from F. Bosselman and D. Callies, *The Quiet Revolution in Land Use Control* (Washington, D.C.: Council on Environmental Quality, 1972).

7. An important measure of this change has been the enthusiastic public response to E.F. Schumacher, *Small Is Beautiful* (New York: Harper and Row, 1973).

8. Rachel Carson, *Silent Spring* (Boston: Houghton Mifflin, 1962); Barry Commoner, *The Closing Circle: Nature, Man, and Technology* (New York: Alfred Knopf, 1971); and Paul Ehrlich, *The Population Bomb* (New York: Ballantine, 1968).

9. A comprehensive review of legal cases and principles involved with zoning that supports my view that zoning is not a way of providing public goods at private expense may be found in J.A. Kusler, "Open Space Zoning: Valid Regulation or Invalid Taking," *Minnesota Law Review* 57 (no. 1) (1972).

3   **Property Rights and Resource Uses**

Any discussion of existing American institutions for the control of land use and the environment must start with a consideration of the existing distribution and definition of property rights. It is our present pattern of property rights that determines the decisions of farmers to sell land to developers for residential subdivisions, which determines the price of land for homes, factories, or parks, the patterns of pollution, and the interpersonal distribution of income.

What has determined the existing definition and distribution of property rights? It is difficult to organize the logic or explanation of the present complex of property rights as they affect land use and the environment for, as Justice Oliver Wendell Holmes once remarked, "The life of the law is not logic but experience." The explanation of why our property institutions have their existing forms must be made in terms of our historical development and the development of particular institutions to meet particular problems of economic and social organization in our past.

Private property rights were not invented by a master planner or legislature. They evolved out of men's experience in trying to organize their activities in a way that was both efficient and equitable. The present corpus of law and practice governing land use has accreted through legislative enactments, judicial decisions, and private contracts. It works—badly, say some. This chapter will explore some of the ways in which private property rights are defined in the organization of land and other resource use.

The rules governing the use of land and the environment are of infinite variety and complexity in our society, as they are in all civilized and complex societies. But from the customs and laws governing agricultural tenure in medieval Europe, to the complex leases on air rights over the London and New York financial districts, the common functions of allocation and distribution are performed by systems of property law in land, space, and natural resources.

Private property and markets could be considered a response to certain basic problems that every society must deal with in the organization of production and its distribution. The problem in production is incentives and efficiency. How can a society get its members to work harder, or create and conserve capital, or allocate resources in such a way as to get more of the goods and services that are desired (and less of the "bads" such as pollution or resource exhaustion that are not desired)?

A second problem is distribution. How can a society distribute income in such a way as to minimize social strife and secure a general consensus that the distribution is fair while at the same time preserving the incentives for production and conservation?

Three general responses to these problems can be distinguished in societies at different stages of development — tradition, the market, and centralized control. Private property is an integral part of a market system because it is property rights that are exchanged in market transactions. If Jones buys land from Smith, he is purchasing the right to use and control that land in certain ways. If Jones rents the land from Smith, he is purchasing the right to use and control land in certain ways for a limited time period.

Traditional or central control systems attempt to deal with the incentive and efficiency problems in production with social sanctions or criminal penalties. An individual in a traditional society who does not perform his status-determined role is disciplined by social pressure or punishment. In a modern central-control system, he may be branded an "enemy of the people" or sent to Siberia. At the same time even in a socialist system, positive incentives in the form of recognition or awards or even cash bonuses may be used to stimulate greater net output.

A private property, market system does not need to rely on *social* incentives or disincentives. Gains or losses to the property holder result from his effective or noneffective management of his assets automatically through the operation of the market. Thus the social costs of enforcing behavior are minimized.

The Functions of Property Rights

In any society the definition and enforcement of property rights and their exchange in the market fulfill five necessary functions. First, property rights reduce conflicts among members of the society as they determine the distribution of income and wealth by allowing certain members of the society to use resources in particular ways for their own purposes. Second, property rights allocate and ration the use of scarce resources between alternative uses. Third, property rights allocate resources between present and future use. Fourth, by vesting the control of resources with an individual (or corporation) and securing his control over the use of resources for a specified and certain future tenure, society gives an incentive to the individual to increase or improve the output available from the resources through the investment of capital or labor in their increased productivity. Fifth, society may also reduce transactions, bureaucratic, and/or enforcement costs by placing these costs on the interested individuals rather than on bureaucratic managers.

The market — private exchange transactions for the sale and rental of property rights — is the basic institution determining the use of land and other natural resources in the United States. Market outcomes are affected and modified by tax laws, zoning, and a variety of regulations and standards. However, it is basically the *individual's* decision that determines land use. It is property rights to use, rent, or sell land that are exchanged in market transactions.

Property rights exist when a society will uphold and enforce the rights of a particular person (or corporation) to use a particular asset in a particular way and prohibit the rest of society from using the asset or interfering with the individual's use and enjoyment of the asset in which he has property rights. A market system in which property rights to the use and control of assets are exchangeable is driven by individual self-interest and controlled by competition.

Income Distribution

Private property in land or other resources is an important determinant of income and wealth distribution. The owner of a square foot of Manhattan or an acre of Iowa can receive a handsome income from the use of his property by himself or others. It has not always been so. The Dutch purchased Manhattan Island from the Indians for $24 in the seventeenth century. Iowa sold for $1 per acre a century ago. Land (and natural resources) only command a market price when they are scarce relative to the capital and labor necessary to develop them.

When America was settled in the seventeenth to nineteenth centuries, there was an abundant supply of land relative to the demand for it. As a consequence, undeveloped land was given away free or sold at nominal prices. The price of unimproved land was kept low by its seemingly unlimited availability. There was abundant land. There was less capital and labor available to utilize it in a productive manner.

Private property in land is an important determinant of income distribution only if the land itself commands an "economic rent" — a surplus over the other costs of production. Land in the desert or the arctic tundra produces no surplus. Its ownership does nothing for the income and wealth of its owner.

Because the development of land and the equalization of income and wealth have been important social objectives in the United States over the past two centuries, the federal government has attempted to secure the widest possible distribution of land ownership by a variety of programs. Following the American Revolution and the Civil War, veterans were given land in payment for wartime military service. In the early nineteenth century, large areas of land were sold in small parcels at low prices. The Homestead Act of 1862 provided for free land to settlers.

In the twentieth century irrigation rights in federal projects were limited to 160 acres per individual in order to spread ownership and benefits more widely. The nonenforcement of this provision is presently a matter of controversy. Perhaps the most effective program ever undertaken by the federal government to encourage the widespread ownership of real estate has been the Federal Housing Administration (FHA) and the Veterans Administration (VA) programs of mortgage insurance that have enabled many Americans to borrow money to purchase their homes.

The wide distribution of land ownership among the population has long been recognized as an important element in political stability and the protection of the interests of the individual against the overweening state power. The Jeffersonian concept of a democratic republic of small landowners has been a powerful force in shaping American policies toward land.

The ownership of land and natural resources has not been as important a determinant of income and wealth distribution in the United States in the past as it has been in some other societies. This difference is both because land ownership is distributed more equally among the U.S. population and because the income from labor and man-made capital assets is a larger proportion of national income in the United States. However, the increasing scarcity of land and natural resources relative to the population may cause significant shifts in the proportion of income accruing to owners of land and resources in the future and make land and resource ownership a more important determinant of income distribution.

Equalization of incomes and equalization of land ownership are a very powerful political issue. Hostility and opposition to definitions and distributions of property rights that enforce great inequality in the ownership of land and other assets are endemic in many societies. They have historically been important in most major revolutions.

The question of great inequalities in land ownership could never be a burning social question in the United States as long as land and natural resources were so abundant relative to the labor and capital necessary to utilize them. In the last decade the increase in the price of land and housing relative to disposable incomes has started to change the prospects for home ownership for a new generation of Americans. Their reaction to this economic and social change is unpredictable.

The only important social reformer and critic to have raised the issue of inequality resulting from land ownership in U.S. history was Henry George, who wrote in the last quarter of the nineteenth century.[1] While he attracted a considerable following, neither his prophesies nor policies were accepted although the logic of his analysis is sound, and his prophesies will be realized to the extent that land is scarce relative to labor and capital.

Efficient Allocation

The second function of private property in resources is allocatory. The sale or rental market for land allocates its use to the highest value and highest bidder. This serves to increase the value of total output for a society.

When an exchange transaction takes place in the marketplace, two sets of property rights are exchanged. If an individual sells his property rights in a parcel of land to someone else, the buyer acquires the rights to use it to build a house or grow potatoes, and the seller receives money that allows him to acquire other goods. Given the basic economic problem of limited resources and unlimited demands, property rights to the use of scarce resources are allocated to the highest bidders. In a system based on private property, the owners of specific assets have an incentive to use them in the way that will produce the highest return or sell them to someone else who will.

Social productivity is increased by rationing the use of scarce assets so that they will be used to produce those goods and services to which society attaches the highest value. If a residential lot in Scarsdale (a high-income suburb of New York City) were used to grow potatoes, there would be a small net return to the owner after the payment for the variable inputs of labor, fertilizer, seed, tractor services, and so on. The small net return would reflect the difference between the price of potatoes and the price of the factors (other than land) used in their production.

If, on the other hand, a house were built on the Scarsdale lot, the annual rental that the owner might charge for its use would be in considerable excess of the annual capital and maintenance charges on the dwelling. Housing space in Scarsdale is highly valued. Private property in land gives the owner a strong economic incentive to use it to produce the goods and services that society values most highly or sell it to someone who will. This is the dynamic that drives the conversion of land from one use to another.

The holder of property rights in scarce assets has an incentive to ensure the socially optimal allocation of those assets through obtaining the maximum price for their use. In the absence of the rationing mechanism that results from property rights — or some administrative surrogate — scarce resources would be used in an inefficient way; that is, net social output, as measured by market prices, could be increased by an allocation of the scarce resources to those who would be willing to pay a higher price for their use.

Intertemporal Allocation

Property rights play a particularly important role in allocating the use of resources between present and future use. The existence of enforceable and secure property rights should result, in theory, in the conservation of resources for future use. Their absence may lead the present possessor to resource consumption and exhaustion today through fear that the resources may be taken by someone else tomorrow.

Most (if not all) of the situations in which conservation is a serious problem result from the absence or insecurity of property rights. Resources where property rights to exclusive use have not been established are sometimes called "open access resources."

Petroleum and natural gas have sometimes been open access resources in the past because it was difficult to attach enforceable property rights to underground reserves — the rights would be attached only to drilling rights on the land surface above the reserves. Unless the person who discovered oil had drilling rights on *all* the surface area over a particular pool of petroleum or natural gas, it would be economically rational for him to pump it all out as fast as possible in order to prevent some other person from doing so before him.

This would have two socially undesirable effects: First, it would prevent the recovery of the petroleum at a rate that would maximize the present value of a discounted stream of returns from the oil. The owner could not afford to wait until some future time when the oil was more highly valued by society because someone else might pump the oil before him. The lower price in the present would encourage more profligate use of the resource by consumers, and it would be unavailable in the future when it was more highly valued.

The absence of property rights in oil pools would also tend to discourage the exploration for and development of new oil reserves since an oil company would have less incentive to explore and develop if other firms could rush in after discovery and drill wells into the pool. The exploring company could protect itself only by acquiring drilling rights over all the land that they expected to overlay an oil pool.

The lack of congruence between property rights on land surface and oil pools has led to a variety of cooperative agreements and governmental controls to limit and allocate production. These, however, are an imperfect surrogate for a set of property rights that would give exclusive access to a scarce resource in that they result in additional expense and are not certain and secure.

Water is another example of the inadequacies of property rights leading to misallocation of resources. The pollution of streams by upstream users may deprive downstream users of valuable uses or impose high treatments costs upon them. Or in other cases pollution control may be enforced on upstream users at a cost above any benefit to downstream users.

In the arid southwestern United States, groundwater is being pumped for agricultural use at a rate that is causing the level of groundwater to subside. This imposes heavier pumping costs on present users and may preclude future use of the underground aquifers. The net value of the water used in producing crops may be quite small and yet the users have no incentive to conserve its use for the future or allocate it to more valuable uses in the present because there are no enforceable and readily transferable rights in groundwater held in underground aquifers.[2]

Fisheries are another example of an open access resource where the absence of exclusive property rights results in inefficiency. The problem with regard to the fisheries, in contrast to oil or water, is complicated by the existence of an unusual biological yield function. The problem of rational use of the resource is similar to the use of land for the growing of forests or grazing. Economic rationality would discourage a landowner from cutting down a forest without replanting or overgrazing rangeland in such a way that the land would be lost for further productive use. Yet with a fishery the economic incentives to maximize the value of the yield from a renewable resource over time leads to overfishing. The individual has no incentive to conserve the stock of fish because, if he does, he has no way to prevent others from taking the fish.

The fisheries problem has been widely recognized as has the problem of mining the ocean seabed. The Law of the Sea conferences, however, have not produced satisfactory international agreements, and in the last several years, as a consequence, nations have been unilaterally extending their claims to sovereign control from the traditional 10 miles to 200 miles.[3]

Within U.S. waters, the problem of the fisheries has been approached with attempts to limit the annual catch by limiting the efficiency of the gear, the time that can be fished, the number of fish that can be taken by one person or boat, and so on. This results always in the inefficient use of capital and labor in fishing (the purpose of the regulation that seeks to limit yield to conserve the stock of fish by promoting inefficiency). The result is higher costs of catching fish through the net loss of productive efficiency. The rational policy would be to limit the human and capital resources involved in fishing but allow the most efficient means of catching fish. The desired amount of fish could be caught with far less labor and capital and the factors of production released could then be diverted to other productive uses.

A surplus, "an economic rent," will accrue to the owner of a fishery, as it accrues to the owner of a forest, if the price of fish exceeds their cost of production by the most efficient means. If the cost of production is driven up to limit the number of fish being caught in order to conserve the fishery, it means that social output falls short of its attainable maximum as resources of capital and labor that could be used elsewhere are used for catching fish by less efficient means. Only treating the fishery resource as if it were private property will assure that this does not happen.[4]

The case of the fisheries points up an important function of property rights. Since economic rents (as will be discussed more fully in chapter 6) occur when the use of certain resources can increase social output and save factors of production, property rights should be preventing the dissipation of economic rent. Indeed, the capture of an economic rent and the avoidance of its dissipation were the motive force that led to the development of property rights in land at the end of the Middle Ages.

The effects of uncertain expectations about the future form of property rights can be seen in recent developments in the state of California in the use of timber and coastal land. The possibility that an increased acreage of redwood forest in northern California will be incorporated into national forests or parks has led to cutting of the lands proposed for condemnation for public use. This indicates an uncertainty upon the part of the owners that the condemnation price would be as great as the market value of the trees. The insecurity of their property rights leads to the consumption of the resource.

The impending passage of the California Coastline Commission Act in 1974 led to rapid development of land on which a building moratorium or possible restrictions and uncertainty about development would be imposed. In the case of both the redwoods and coastal lands, uncertainties about the future security of private property led to what was probably a premature (and inefficient) use of land and forest resources.

Another illustration of the effects of a lack of property rights on the behavior of property owners can be seen in the results of a government housing program in the early 1970s—the "HUD 235" program. Under this program low-income families were enabled to "buy" homes at inflated prices for virtually no downpayment other than minimum closing costs. Interest on the monthly payments on the mortgages was subsidized. Because "owners" had no equity in the houses—in fact, the mortgage was frequently greater than the real market value of the house—many families allowed their payments to lapse and the properties to deteriorate until they were evicted after a statutory period during which they had in effect lived rent-free.

The behavior was economically rational on their part since their claims on the use of the resource were less than the claims against them for its use. From a social point of view, the lack of property rights led to deterioration in the value of assets.

Productivity

The fourth function of property rights is the provision of incentives to members of a society to increase the availability and productivity of resources. If a man has property in his own labor, he has an incentive to use it productively for his own welfare. Free men work harder and more efficiently than slaves. They have property in the results of their labor. If men have property rights in capital, they have an inducement to save from present consumption to create capital. If they can have private property in land and resources, they have a powerful incentive to develop and conserve the productivity of those resources.

The inevitability of some social definition of property rights to distribute income is fairly obvious. The usefulness of property rights in promoting efficiency in asset allocation is evident upon examination of the operation of markets and the problems that result from the absence of property claims to open access assets. The effectiveness of property rights in minimizing transactions and enforcement costs in the social organization of resources is plausible.

The social utility of property rights as an incentive for increasing the quantity and productivity of natural resources is not intuitively obvious and bears further examination to identify the conditions under which property rights in land and other natural resources create an improved situation for society as a whole (as opposed to the individual who gets the property rights in the natural resources).

Why should a particular individual be granted property rights in land by the rest of society? Do such rights make him "richer" and the rest of society "poorer" as part of what was previously held in common passes to private ownership? Is it not true, as the French philosopher Proudhon wrote, that "private property is robbery from the common possession of mankind"?

The social utility of private property depends on the quantity of goods and services available to society, after the vesting of property rights in an individual member of that society, being greater for the rest of society, *ex-individual,* than before the vesting of the property rights, or in their absence.[5]

Consider the matter closely. Suppose that a hypothetical society had 10 members and 10 acres of land that were "owned" and worked in common with the output being divided equally. Then suppose that one member of the society proposed that he be allowed to withdraw from the communal arrangements, forfeiting his rights to communal consumption and removing 1 acre from common ownership.

The remaining 9 members of society would be as well off as before if they were dividing the output of 9 acres and 9 men among 9 consumers. They would have a positive incentive to consent to the arrangement only if they were able to acquire some of the increased output from the acre worked by its sole proprietor by trading with him or taxing him for some of the increase in output. He would have the incentive to seek the arrangement only if the gains were large enough to compensate him for the trouble of securing property rights, accepting the greater risks, and yielding part of his surplus back to the rest of society through exchange of goods and services or through taxes.

It is of crucial importance to note that it is only when property rights increase the productivity of resources *and* society gets part of the gain that the creation of private property in resources leaves all members of society better off than they would otherwise be—to use the terminology of economists, the result is "Pareto-optimal." (A variant of this rule for the principles determining property rights will be found in the "maximin" or "difference principle" of John Rawls found in the next chapter.)

Transactions Costs

Clearly defined systems of property rights reduce the costs of negotiation and enforcement in the organization of economic activity. Many economists have explained the evolution of forms of land ownership or industrial organization in terms of legal arrangements to reduce costs of management and control. Thus feudal land tenure is viewed as less efficient than freehold property, partnerships are viewed as less efficient than general-purpose, chartered, limited-liability corporations, and zoning ordinances are viewed as more efficient than restrictive covenants or nuisance law. All the judgments about efficiency are made in terms of reductions of the negotiation and enforcement costs of individuals. Efficiency is a compelling argument for individual property rights. It has been extensively discussed in the economic literature.

Environmental Problems and Property Rights

It can be argued that the instances in which the market fails to produce satisfactory outcomes, that is, outcomes that are "inefficient" or "inequitable," are situations in which property rights are poorly defined or competition is impaired or inoperative. Let us consider this explanation of "market failure" in terms of some examples of types of land-use problems cited in chapter 1.

The first category of criticisms urged against our present system of institutions controlling land use and the environment is that they are "wasteful and inefficient." Some examples of waste and inefficiency cited include the cutting of forests, the development of agricultural land, and the urban sprawl that results in larger expenditures on roads and public utility systems.

What determines the decision of an individual or corporation to cut down a forest? If we presume rational self-interest in the maximization of wealth and income, the decision will be made when the value of the flow of services of the forest resource is maximized. Considering only the value of the timber, the trees will be cut when to wait longer would produce a smaller discounted present value for the forest assets.

If we assume the relative prices established by markets to be a reliable indicator of social valuation of timber now versus timber in the future, then the decision of the owner of the forest to cut at a particular time will be identical with the social interest in the maximization of value from the forest resource over time.

There are, however, a number of complications. Suppose that in addition to timber, the forest provides the public with woodland walks, visual amenity, stabilization of stream flow, and even modification of the hydrologic cycle, temperature modification, and the conversion of carbon dioxide to oxygen in photosynthesis. These services are all extremely valuable to society as provided by the forest resource but the property rights of the owner do not extend in such a way that he can impose a charge on the public for these services. (Conceivably, the owner might be able to charge various use fees, but the costs of collecting them present insurmountable costs and practical difficulties. There are also reasons, associated with the zero marginal cost of these services, that it would be undesirable to have any restrictions on these uses (woodland walks, visual amenity) if they could be physically controlled.) He therefore does not take them into account in a calculation of when and how to maximize the return from the management of the forest resource. It is the incomplete coverage of property rights, in this instance, that leads to a decision in which the interests of the individual owner of the forest and the public are not synonymous.

The management of forests provides an interesting example of the development of social controls over resource use over time. Medieval forests were "managed" by the allocation of particular uses in a controlled manner through a series of "privileges." The lord of the manor might have the privilege of hunting in the forest while the peasants could graze animals and gather firewood there. Freehold ownership with exclusive use came only when the value of the land for agricultural purposes or the value of the forest for timber or charcoal made it economically advantageous for individuals to undertake the expense of converting the forests to freehold tenure.

In the nineteenth-century United States, forests and land were so plentiful that the establishment and enforcement of property rights in forests were not particularly important. As a consequence, the federal government entered the twentieth century with substantial ownership of forest, prairie, desert, and other nonagricultural land. In recent years the management of public lands by the Forest Service, Bureau of Land Management, and National Park Service has attempted to take into account the multiple uses of forest and other land.

This of course does not solve the allocation problem — intertemporal trade-offs in the timing of timber harvesting must still be made as well as trade-offs among timber, recreation, and watershed functions. The difficulties of organizing markets for particular kinds of property rights leaves decisions about the allocation and distribution of particular resource uses to nonmarket mechanisms. The use of forest lands owned by the government has become a political football contested by many interest groups.

Another frequently cited example of market failure creating a need for land-use planning is urban sprawl. Two kinds of inefficiency are involved here. One is the alleged intertemporal inefficiency that will result from the virtually irreversible conversion of agricultural land to urban use. The other is the waste of capital on the construction of roads, sewers, and other utility systems over a large area when they could be more efficiently concentrated by more intensive development.

The decision of a landowner to convert agricultural land to residential or industrial use will take place when the anticipated net rents from developed uses of the land exceed those from less-developed ones. These rents are the market measure of the value of land in different uses. (See chapter 6.)

From a social point of view, preventing the conversion of agricultural land to industrial use would decrease the value of social output (see chapter 6) if the rents would be larger in developed than undeveloped uses. There is a *prima facie* case for believing that conversion is a rational decision from the individual owner's point of view and the social point of view.

There are, however, several circumstances in which this would not be so. Land developers might not correctly anticipate the future level of rents from agricultural use resulting from higher food prices in the future. The more likely reason for the divergence of the individual and social valuation of the land in agricultural use, however, may be the inability of the property owner to establish property rights in certain benefits conferred on society by the existence of agricultural land — visual amenity, and so on.

It will be argued in subsequent chapters, however, that the problem of urban sprawl (if it is a problem) is substantially increased by distortions induced by public policies governing taxation, zoning, and public utilities rather than market failure caused by the lack of appropriate property rights.

In terms of the first argument for land-use planning — the waste and inefficiency in the use of resources resulting from the failure of the market to account for valuable benefits conferred on nonowners — the problem is the absence or incompleteness of property rights in what could be considered "public goods."

The defining characteristic of public goods is that their consumption or (enjoyment) by one member of society does not reduce the quantity or quality left for others. The recreation, visual amenity, stream-flow stabilization, or even climate moderation provided by forest or agricultural land near urban areas are valuable benefits furnished to society for which the owners of the resources cannot establish and enforce property rights and, consequently, cannot charge.

The continuation of these social benefits do have a cost to the owners and to society in terms of the alternative benefits foregone by nonutilization of the resources. The cost of preserving forest as a park by not cutting the trees is the lumber foregone; the cost of retaining land in agricultural production is the value of residential housing precluded from the site. The problem inherent in private ownership of public goods is the inability of the private owner to balance public benefits with private costs.

The second category of problems distinguished in the opening chapter was the *adverse* effects of particular land uses—pollution being the prime example. Just as waste and inefficiency, from a social point of view, may arise from the failure of the market to take into account certain *benefits* conferred on nonowners of resources which their owners cannot take into account, social welfare may be severely damaged because individual decision makers do not have to take into account the adverse effects of their resource use on other members of society.

The noxious smog that blankets many cities arises from the lack of property rights in the air. The noise of airports persists because airplane passengers and airline companies have been able to make the population surrounding airports bear the costs of noise. If airport neighbors could establish property rights in a measure of tranquility in their own homes, they could force the reduction of airport noise (or its relocation). It is the *de facto* lack of property rights in air, water, and soundwaves that shifts many of the distasteful aspects of modern life onto the general population.

It is important to notice in the cases just considered the conceptual impossibility of distinguishing between the conferral of a benefit and the withdrawal of a cost.[7] Does the owner of a forest confer a benefit in the stabilization of stream flow or a cost when he cuts the forest and causes floods? From a social point of view, the cost of stable stream flow is the lumber foregone and part of the cost of the lumber is the destabilized stream flow.

It is important to notice the nature and incidence of costs and benefits from resource use. From a social point of view resources have many alternative uses, and their valuation depends on the abundance of the resources relative to the demands for them. Forest land may be used for lumber production. Or it may be maintained in a natural condition for visual amenity and environmental effects. Or it may be converted to agricultural or residential use. The air may be enjoyed in its natural state, or it may be used to dissipate sound and industrial waste. A poor society may define property rights to increase lumber production while a rich society may define property to maintain forests as parks.

Any use of the environment has both costs and benefits that must be balanced. When costs and benefits cannot be internalized by a decision maker, his decision in terms of personal costs and benefits may be different from the rest of society.

As soon as resources are scarce relative to the demands made on them by different people for different uses, property rights must be established to allocate uses among persons. Property rights do this by internalizing costs and benefits for the property owner. It was the need to internalize costs and benefits and reduce the transaction and enforcement costs of resource management that led to the development of private property in land at the end of the Middle Ages when land started to become scarce relative to labor and capital.

The fragmented and interdependent ways in which property rights to the use of resources are defined contributes to the problem. Take the forest land example again. If one individual controlled all the benefits of the forest, his decision to cut timber would be made only if the net proceeds he received from the sale of the timber were greater than the payments the rest of society would be willing to pay him to leave it forested so they could enjoy the resulting environmental effects.

Even so there are a number of impediments to the latter outcome. The forest owner would have to negotiate payments from a large number of individuals, all of whom would have an interest in understating the environmental values of the forest to them and allowing everyone else to pay for the benefit that they would continue to enjoy even if they had not paid. High transaction costs and the "free-rider" problem militate against a socially optimal result if it must be negotiated by all members of society with a single owner who possesses the property rights that enable him to raze the forest.

There are several alternatives. Suppose that the forest were owned by a government that is able to establish some estimate of the monetary value of the environmental amenity conferred by the forest on society as a whole. In this instance, a rational decision (assuming a rational and social utility-maximizing government) to harvest the forest would be taken only when the price offered for the right to harvest exceeded the estimated value of the environmental amenity.

Consider a second alternative. Suppose that the forest is owned by an individual but that the government undertakes to negotiate the interests of society as a whole in the environmental amenities by paying the owner not to harvest. The cost of lumber must now explicitly recognize the environmental amenity foregone as an opportunity cost since the private owner would not harvest if the payments receivable for maintenance of the forest exceeded the profit from sale of the lumber. The same principles applicable to the preservation of a forest could be applied to the analysis of land-use decisions for agricultural land, sea coasts, or other areas of natural beauty or environmental interest.

Two inferences may be made from these alternative arrangements for organizing choices about resource use. First, if the benefits from a resource are diffuse, the use of a market in the exchange of property rights in a resource use is likely to produce an inefficient allocation of resource uses because of high transaction costs and the "free-rider" problem.

Second, if this "market failure" is remedied by collective action for the valuation of the diffuse environmental amenities, the optimal decision in terms of maximizing value from the resource use will be the same regardless of whether an individual or the government has property rights in the resource. The difference will be the distribution of income after the allocation has been made with the party possessing the property rights receiving the payment or foregoing the payment for the resource use—be it timber or environmental amenity. (This is another illustration of the Coase principle discussed in chapter 1.)

The same point may be demonstrated in a slightly different way with the noise pollution from airports. If the airlines have de facto property rights to the use of the air for the dissipation of sound, they need not install noise-reducing modifications to engines, locate airports on blocks of land large enough to mitigate the problem, subsidize soundproofing for neighboring residents of airports, or compensate neighboring residents for the infliction of noise. Airline users will be paying lower costs for air-transportation services, and airport neighbors will be subjected to a reduction in their quality of life by noise.

If, on the other hand, residential property rights were to be defined to include freedom from noise above a certain level in a person's home, then airlines would incur a variety of costs to mitigate noise that would be passed on to airline users in the form of higher use charges. Airport neighbors would then not have to bear the psychic costs of noise or the monetary costs of accoustical treatment to lower the noise level.

Suppose that airlines are not responsible for their noise (a variant of the current situation in which there are some standards on decibel levels). There is nothing to stop the residents neighboring the airports from paying the airlines to reduce noise except the transaction costs and the free-rider problem. Or suppose that the airlines may not violate the property rights of the nearby residents in some standard level of low noise pollution. The airlines could compensate the residents for the continuing use of their property. *If* there were zero (or equal) transaction costs associated with the assignment to either party of property rights to the use of the air, the cost-minimizing, utility-maximizing solution to the use of the airwaves would arise no matter how the property rights were allocated. Only the distribution of costs and benefits from the solution would differ.

It could be argued that the airport residents have already been compensated for the costs of noise by the lower land values attaching to houses in the airport vicinity. This argument, however, speaks only to the distributional aspect of the noise cost as the reduction of land values only indicates the dissipation of values that would otherwise obtain but for the noise.

It is a substantial social loss and an inefficient outcome if a million-dollar loss from noise damage (as measured by rent diminution) could be overcome by a thousand-dollar expenditure on noise reduction. It would equally be a social loss if a million dollars were expended to decrease noise inflicting only a thousand-dollar loss from noise damage.

The Historical Relativity of Property Rights

The present distribution and definition of property rights in land and natural resources in the United States evolved to meet the substantial demand for particular kinds of commodities and services. Our pressing needs in the past were not forests for the provision of environmental amenity but wood for houses and ships and agricultural land for the production of crops. Unrestricted individual control of particular parcels of land was a means of stimulating investment in its transformation for the production of goods, assuring its allocation to the production of goods that would command the highest returns in markets.

The third problem necessitating land-use planning cited in the opening chapter was the preservation of natural areas. This matter has already been touched on in terms of the benefits conferred by forest and agricultural land. The use of natural areas, like the use of air, water, or solitude presents an entirely different set of considerations for resource management than those property rights are usually established to deal with.

One person's nonconsumptive use of air, water, solitude, or wilderness does *not* preclude its use by others. From a social point of view, if the incremental cost of one person's use of a lake or forest or seashore is zero (there is no reduction in the value of use by others), then there is no logic to limiting his use of the resource by the imposition of a use fee. If there is no reason to limit nonconsumptive use, then there is no need for individual exclusive property rights that allow an owner to exclude other users.

What is needed for the protection of wilderness is its protection from *consumptive* uses. The public had less need in the past to establish public property in nonconsumptive use of air, water, or wilderness because consumptive use did not diminish, to any appreciable extent, the amount remaining.

One way to understand the implications and relativity of the present structure of property rights in land is to consider an alternative structure used by a different society for dealing with the problems of resource allocation and income distribution. The medieval arrangements that preceded the development of market capitalism, and particularly freehold ownership of land, illustrate some of the significant functions played by property rights in our management of natural resources.[8]

Medieval economic organization depended on an overlapping set of status-determined privileges and obligations. Conceptually, the system was based on the theory that the monarch served as God's agent in the management of all the land and labor in a particular realm. The king allocated the use of land and the use of serfs among his vassals. King, vassal, and serf all owed each other certain duties and possessed certain privileges. Vassals and serfs had privileges in the use of land, but they could not sell or dispose of their privileges to others without the consent of their feudal superior. Privileges and obligations were personal and not transferable.[9]

The privilege of using land carried with it the obligation to render certain services and fees to one's feudal superior. The vassals had to furnish military services to the king. The serfs had to render labor on the manorial estate and certain payments of crops at various times of the year. From an exchange point of view, the privileges were exactly offset by the obligations, and there were no net asset values in use privileges to be sold.

Much of the arable land on the feudal manor was farmed cooperatively because of existing technology. The feudal lords had privileges to hunt in the forests while the serfs had privileges to gather firewood and graze animals there. The arable fields were tilled in common because of the necessity of pooling draft animals and equipment for plowing. While fields were plowed cooperatively, they were harvested in strips by individuals—usually in proportion to their contribution to the plow teams. After harvest, animals were grazed on the fields—in part to manure them and restore some of their fertility. The common use of the same land by a social group was economically rational, that is, it maximized output, with given technology and resource availability.

Cooperative land-use systems were admirably suited to medieval technology and the abundance of land relative to labor and capital to work it. The cooperative medieval system of land tenure began to be replaced by freehold land tenure of specific parcels for a variety of reasons. Most important was the accumulation of capital in the form of draft animals and plows by particular individuals who could therefore opt out of communal arrangements for plowing.

Vassalage became less important for the provision of military services to the monarch, and more important as a source of revenue to allow the monarch to finance military forces and royal expenditures. Feudal dues were increasingly converted into cash payments as were the feudal dues payable from the serf to his manorial overlord. Feudal dues were ended in England in 1660 by a parliamentary act that granted the monarch, in return for their abolishment, the right to tax the sale of alcoholic beverages.

Feudal land tenure had three important disadvantages: uncertainty, high transactions costs, and inability of the individual to limit costs and capture benefits from more efficient resource use. Let us consider these factors in turn.

One of the greatest drawbacks of feudal tenure was the uncertainty and fear of arbitrary action by one's feudal superior. Since the vassals, in theory, held their privileges in land tenure at the pleasure of the king, their feudal dues and obligations could be increased at his pleasure, or he could take their land from them and settle it on another vassal. It was precisely the arbitrary use of royal power to do this that led to the Magna Carta of 1216 in England, which was an agreement between monarch and vassals that he would not arbitrarily deprive them of their feudal privileges. By the eighteenth century most of the heirs and assigns of the former feudal holders of land had transmuted their feudal tenure to freehold.

The other defect of the uncertainty and insecurity of land holding was remedied contractually between the landlords and their feudal inferiors over a long period of time. Certain rich serfs purchased freehold tenure of certain parcels of land within the manor and extinguished any claims on themselves or their land by their feudal overlord.

The substitution of secure and absolute freehold tenure for the insecurity of feudal tenure made land a valuable, transferable, and negotiable asset. Individuals now had an economic incentive to improve the productivity of land by drainage and fencing because they knew they would reap the benefits from increased productivity as income or capital gains. Individual owners who lacked the means or interest in land improvement were bought out by those who could improve it.

The political and social consequences of freehold tenure in land were enormous. A man's economic security no longer depended on the forbearance of the monarch or his feudal superior. Political freedom is inseparable from economic independence. Freehold tenure meant that individuals had the protection of the courts for the security of their economic assets. Privileges were turned into property rights.[10]

The second important consequence of the substitution of freehold tenure for the overlapping system of status-determined privileges and obligations in land use was the reduction of transaction costs. One of the great problems of cooperative resource use was the time and energy involved in getting agreements about which crops to plant, when to plow, which days would be devoted to road building, and so on. While the reduction of all interpersonal arrangements about cooperation in production to a cash nexus may have its disadvantages socially, psychologically, or ethically, it has some substantial offsetting advantages in efficient organization and planning.

The third consequence of the creation of freehold tenure in land was the development of a radically new framework for the resolution of conflicts of interest between members of a society in resource allocation and income distribution. Freehold property in land internalized both the costs and benefits of land use.

An example may make this clear. A common field in medieval tenure furnished benefits in the form of crops and pasturage for various manorial residents in terms of elaborately arranged sharing agreements. An increase in effort or efficiency worked out by one member of the manorial community would increase the benefits for all, but the individual's share of the increase in benefits might be small in proportion to his efforts.

There was also the problem of overgrazing on common fields or premature cutting of trees in common forests. The individual had an incentive to increase the number of animals grazing a common field even though this might lead to a decrease in total yield through overgrazing. His increase in yield from additional animals was less than the present and future losses of yield from the effects of overgrazing on all the animals kept on the common land.

Collective use of the commons resulted in its overgrazing and the cutting of the forests. Every member of the manor had an individual interest in grazing an additional animal or cutting an additional tree, even though the social costs of doing this were greater, in terms of the reduction of output, than the individual benefit received. Individual benefit was greater than individual cost even though individual benefit was less than the social cost inflicted on the rest of society.

The problems of medieval land tenure were solved by the substitution of freehold ownership (private property) of land. They could have been solved by the elaboration of rules for continuing common ownership to account for the problems, but private property emerged because of lower negotiation and enforcement costs. Private property in land increased the security of tenure by making land use by an individual a right rather than a privilege. The benefits of improved productivity on the old open fields were *internalized* by rescinding the claims of other members of the manor on increased output. The superiority of private over collective ownership of land in terms of incentives resulted because the individual cost/individual benefit ratio became the same as the social cost/social benefit ratio.

In England the common lands were enclosed, that is, converted to freehold tenure, by negotiated agreements among the former feudal holders of privileges to use the commons or by parlimentary acts (or by force). This internalized the costs of overgrazing or overcutting the land on the individual whose individual cost/individual benefit ratio now became the same as the social cost/social benefit ratio.[11]

The internalization of benefits from increased productivity that resulted from substituting the rights of freehold property for the status system of feudalism had two important effects: First, it increased the incentives for individuals to increase agricultural output by investment in land improvement and increased labor effort. Second, the internalization of costs, forcing decision makers to bear the costs of their actions, led to more efficient use of resources. The former serf who grazed too many animals on his field now had to take into account the effect of grazing an additional cow on the milk and meat production of his other cows and on the productivity of the grassland the following year. To put the matter in economic terms, the individual owner had the incentive to combine the variable factors of production—labor and capital—with the land to produce the largest net output (or economic rent) possible and to maximize the present value of the land by managing it in a way that would produce the greatest possible stream of rents in the future as well.

It is the nature of a private property system to internalize some of the costs and benefits of using an asset such as land. It is the failure of our present system of private property to internalize some of the costs such as pollution and to internalize some of the benefits to others such as visual amenities that leads to problems.

There is the additional consideration of the transactions, negotiation, and enforcement costs of operating a system of cooperative production that must be taken into account. Once again, to use our medieval example, the number of days that each member of the manor would give to the plowing and the tillage of the lord's land were matters for negotiation, and then there had to be enforcement. These costs grew greater as individual incentives to avoid costs and appropriate benefits at social expense increased. Private property was seen as a way of reducing transaction and enforcement costs by making each individual responsible for his own use of land, labor, and capital.

It is informative to observe the rules and regulations of a society in which individual property rights are *not* granted to see the differences in behavior that result. The Soviet Union has reluctantly allowed its citizens to keep and sell the produce of small garden plots in order to stimulate food production. The determination has been made that without this concession to private property in land, both those who raise and those who purchase the food would have less. Soviet citizens are also allowed to save their money to buy apartments or small country cottages (dachas). Once again the assumption is that in the absence of the incentive to save there would be less housing for all.

The Soviet Union also recognizes the responsibility of every citizen to work for the state. This is another way of expressing Soviet citizens' lack of property in their own labor. One of the consequences of this is the nonrecognition of the Soviet citizen's right to emigrate and the Iron Curtain that walls people in. Why should skilled workers or professionals be allowed to flee to Western Europe or to Israel? If their productive contribution to the Soviet Union is greater than their share of consumption, their departure will leave all the members of Soviet society who are left behind "worse off." Is not part of their skill and productivity the result of the Soviet educational system? Why should other societies or the would-be emigrants be allowed to take educationally created skill and productivity with them? Is that not a form of robbery? Should they be allowed to emigrate if they compensate the state for the removal of a share of human capital invested in them by other members of society?

Man does not create land or natural resources. But his enhancement of their productivity by the use of his labor or capital makes them productive, which has traditionally been the moral and practical argument for private property in land. But the moral or practical argument for private property in land or natural resources really extends only to the *increase* in productivity for which the individual granted property rights in that increase is responsible. To allow *more* than that is really to leave less for the rest of society and is difficult to justify on either practical or Pareto-optimal grounds.

Summary

It is time to recapitulate and summarize our discussion of the functions of private property in land and other natural resources. Private property performs a distributional function — it determines income shares for society. This is of small importance when little economic surplus, "economic rent," accrues to the owners of land but will take on increasing importance with the increasing share of rents in national income.

Hypothetically, all rents could be collected by the state through state ownership of resources or through taxation and could be redistributed through subsidies. Both the pattern of income distribution and the means of distribution might be modified by a society. The distributional function of property rights in land could be modified and has been modified in our society by taxation and subsidy.

Private property does provide a necessary allocational function in the organization of economic activity. Private property creates an incentive for the owner to use or sell property rights in land for the uses most highly valued by society. But two points bear emphasis here. First, the utility of private property for efficient allocation is not an argument for any particular distribution of property rights. It is only an argument for their clear definition and easy transferability from one use and one owner to another.

The argument for the sale of property rights in free markets to the "highest and best use" and to the highest bidder to assure allocational efficiency is not an argument for the private retention of the economic rents that result. The owners of commercial land in Manhattan would continue to have an economic incentive to devote it to its highest and best use even if all returns over and above a normal return to capital and management expertise were taxed away. The owner of Iowa farmland would continue to raise corn rather than weeds even if part of the surplus over the costs of production were taxed away. The Texan oil field owner would continue to explore for and pump petroleum as long as the returns on the capital invested give him a normal return adjusted for risk.

It is only the argument for the incentives from increased productivity that constitutes a valid argument for a specific definition and distribution of property rights. Society has an interest in guaranteeing the rights of private property in a piece of farmland to the particular farmer who invests his labor, capital, and knowledge in increasing its productivity by prudent management over the long run. And the same is true for oil fields, urban land, rivers and groundwater, forests, and factory sites.

Property rights do not arise from nature but from social needs, and their form and distribution will be determined by social values and objectives. The logic of private property and the use of the market to allocate resources and distribute income are at the foundation of our system of economic organization. Although our belief in Adam Smith's invisible hand is subject to considerable reservation, there still is a strong underlying belief in the ability of market forces, appropriately modified, to organize economic activities.

We have seen that there are several important qualifications to the proposition that private control over land use will result in the greatest social benefits for the greatest number of people both now and in the future. One qualification comes from the existence of costs that certain uses of land can inflict on other members of society against their wishes. A related qualification comes from the benefits that certain uses of land may provide to other members of society for which an owner cannot charge.

These qualifications to individual and social maximization offered by private property in land are called "externalities." The costs to neighbors of the garbage dump are external to the garbage dump owners. The benefits from the forest to downstream water users from the watershed and to picnickers and hikers are external to the owners of the forest. External costs and benefits are not calculated by the owners in their calculation of the value of land use, and thus their decision about the best use of land to maximize their income and wealth may not reflect the highest total value of a particular use of land to society after the addition and subtraction of external costs and benefits. External benefits and costs are not external to society — only to the calculations of individual owners of limited property rights to resources that have uses that affect others. All benefits have offsetting costs in the benefits foregone from one use to obtain another.

Prohibiting landowners from imposing external costs on others or requiring that they continue to provide external benefits without compensation is often proposed by environmentalists as good public policy. Whether or not it is good public policy may depend on who is paying the costs and who is enjoying the benefits. Should the owners of homes built next to a garbage dump cause the relocation of a municipal garbage dump even though the relocation would impose very large costs on taxpayers—larger than the compensated condemnation of the houses? Should the owner of a forest be forbidden to cut it because it would deprive hikers and picnickers of a park or cause downstream water users to increase their water-storage capacity? These are not easy questions.

There is a final qualification to the proposition that private property in land and resources will lead to "the greatest good for the greatest number." This proposition rests on the assumption that market prices are an adequate and appropriate measure of the value received by all individuals from land use *and* that the value of every dollar of income or expenditure to different individuals are comparable.

There are difficult problems of income distribution and certainty of expectations that must be taken into account in the development of an overall policy to govern land use. There is more to political economy than efficiency. Equity and security from arbitrary charge are also important values to be considered.

Land-use policies are not neutral in their operation. They are not just concerned with development or environmental protection, with efficiency, or with conservation. They are concerned with the *distribution* of income, wealth, and power. Thus any consideration of the institutions involved with private property and governmental regulations on the use of land involve a consideration of the most basic assumptions about the proper role of the state and the relationship of the individual to the state in the definition and enforcement of property rights. To those beliefs and assumptions, we must turn our attention.

Notes

1. Henry George, *Progress and Poverty* (New York: 1883) (Modern Library Edition, 1940).

2. For an extensive discussion, see Maurice M. Kelso, William E. Martin, and Lawrence E. Mack, *Water Supplies and Economic Growth in an Arid Environment* (Tucson, Ariz.: University of Arizona Press, 1973).

3. A wide-ranging discussion of the management of ocean resources may be found in Ross D. Eckert, *The Enclosure of Ocean Resources* (Stanford, Calif.: Hoover Institution Press, 1979).

4. James Crutchfield and Giulio Pontecorvo, *The Pacific Salmon Fisheries: A Study of Irrational Conservation* (Baltimore: Johns Hopkins Press for Resources for the Future, 1969).

5. This argument is made in more formal terms in Gordon C. Bjork, *Private Enterprise and Public Interest: The Development of American Capitalism* (Englewood Cliffs, N.J.: Prentice-Hall, 1969), chap. 5.

6. See E. Furubotn and S. Pejovich, "Property Rights and Economic Theory: A Survey of Recent Literature," *Journal of Economic Literature* 10 (no. 4) (December 1972): 1137-1162.

7. See R.H. Coase, "The Problem of Social Cost," *Journal of Law and Economics* 3 (October 1960).

8. For a classic discussion, see Marc Bloch, *Feudal Society* (London: Routledge and Kegan Paul Ltd., 1961), chap. 18-20, 23.

9. Walter Ullman, *The Individual and Society in the Middle Ages* (Baltimore: Johns Hopkins University Press, 1966).

10. See R.H. Tawney, *Religion and the Rise of Capitalism* (New York: The New American Library, 1960).

11. A classical account of the importance of the enclosures and the importance of internalizing the costs of using natural resources will be found in Garrett Hardin, "The Tragedy of the Commons," *Science* 162 (1968).

The Philosophical Bases of Property Rights in Land

There is nothing which so generally . . . engages the affections of mankind (as that) sole and despotic dominion which one man claims and exercises over the external things of the world, in total exclusion of the right of any other individual in the universe . . . . And yet there are very few, that will give themselves the trouble to consider the original and foundation of these rights . . . . Pleased as we are with the possession, we seem afraid to look back to the means by which it was acquired, as if fearful of some defect in our title, . . . not caring to reflect that (accurately and strictly speaking) there is no foundation in nature or in natural law, why a set of words upon parchment should convey the dominion of land: why the son should have a right to exclude his fellow-creatures from a determinate spot of ground, because his father had done so before him: or why the occupier of a particular field or of a jewel, when lying on his death-bed, and no longer able to maintain possession, should be entitled to tell the rest of the world which of them should enjoy it after him . . . . (Nevertheless) it is well if the mass of mankind will obey the laws when made, without scrutinizing too nicely into the reasons of making them.[1]

Property rights have two very important organizational functions in any society; they are traded in markets to allocate resources between alternative uses; and they serve to distribute the costs and benefits of resource use between individuals. The Coase principle illustrates that (under restrictive conditions) the allocation of property rights to one party or another does not affect the purposes or the efficiency with which resources are used — only the distribution of costs and benefits.[2] Thus the distributional question can be clearly separated from the efficiency question in the analysis of property rights.

What principles are used to explain and justify the interpersonal distribution of property rights in a society? Because land-use planning is directed both at changing the interpersonal distribution of property rights *and* changing the locus and basis for the definition and distribution of property rights, it is important to understand what people *believe* to be the moral, practical, and/or persuasive arguments or theories upon which distribution of property rights are based. Blackstone's recommendations to avoid "scrutinizing too nicely" the basis for property rights will not be accepted by "the mass of mankind" in our time.

All societies develop important and powerful myths and beliefs about the relationship between man and the land. The United States is no exception. This relationship is celebrated in poetry, philosophy, and political rhetoric and embodied in the law, custom, and behavior of the American people. No scheme that ignores the reality of deep-seated beliefs about the proper relationship of man to the land can be politically viable. This is perhaps one of the reasons why the high hopes for land-use planning that flourished in the early seventies did not come to fruition.

Historically, the Jeffersonian concept of America as a democratic republic of small, land-owning farmers and artisans has been a powerful ideological force in shaping American attitudes to governmental policy on land-use questions. The philosophic background of these concepts for Jefferson was eighteenth-century rationalism, but those ideals have been supported, merged, modified, and amplified by many philosophic theories of social organization.

Three Categories of Theories

I would like to distinguish three general categories of theories about the basis of property rights; I will label these three categories *personality*, *social contractarian* or *utilitarian*, and *psychological*. There are no clearly drawn boundaries to these categories, and it is frequently possible to find elements of several of these categories in the ideas of one author or to explain legislation or practice in terms of more than one of the theories. Nevertheless, their distinction is useful for our purposes.

Personality Theories of Property

One approach to social organization emphasizes the origin of property rights in men's personal, creative activity. The classic statement of the personality theory may be found in John Locke's *Second Treatise on Civil Government*.[3] Locke's basic premise is that it is self-evident that a man has a natural right to his life and liberty. He then posits that the exercise of these rights gives him derived rights to anything that is created by the exercise of life and liberty.

The basic premise of Locke's argument was that it was self-evident that every man had property *in himself*. This was a basic premise for the freedom of the individual (and was, of course, in basic opposition to the medieval concept of man, which saw him as an interdependent member of society who could not act without considering the consequences of his actions for other members of society.)

Locke argued that since a man had property in his own person, and the liberty to use his physical and mental powers, the results of the exercise of those powers should also be the property of the individual. If the exercise of these powers created assets, then the assets belonged to their creator.

Property in land created some problems for Locke's argument that property in a loaf of bread or wooden chair created by the exercise of a man's labor did not. While a loaf of bread or wooden chair was obviously created by a man's labor and would not exist without it, land, patently, was not.

Locke used the metaphor of a man "mixing his labor" with land as the basis for the establishment of property rights in land. What Locke had in mind here was the creation of value by the exercise of labor. The *value* in land was created by the human effort of clearing, ditching, draining, or enclosing it. Just as the materials in a loaf of bread or wooden chair had less usefulness or value before their transformation by human skill or effort, land had less value before the investment of human labor in its transformation to more productive use.

One of the problems that Locke's defense of property had to contend with in his own time was the distributional consequences of vesting property rights with one individual rather than another. How could it be moral, the medieval critics of private property in land argued, for one man to alienate into private possession the land that had previously been the common possession of mankind? In addition, what would happen to future generations when all the good land had been alienated into private ownership and some men had none with which to "mix their labor"?

These criticisms, of course, go to the core of the distributional problem. Locke advanced two arguments in reply. He conceded that private alienation of land from common possession could leave the rest of society "worse off," but he tried to argue a specific case in which it did not. He argued that the increase in productivity from private alienation and improvement would leave society, *as a whole*, much better off. The argument has been evaluated in chapter 3.

With respect to the argument that one man's alienation of land precluded other individuals and successive generations from doing the same, Locke attempted to split the problem into two parts: initial acquisition and transferral. The initial acquisition, argued Locke, took place when land was so plentiful that one man's alienation of land into private ownership left "as much and as good" for others. The famous "Lockean proviso" was that so long as the initial alienation of natural resources left no less for others, the initial acquisition was fair. The failure of some men to exercise their freedom to use their labor to acquire land was a result of their sloth or bad judgment. At any event, the initial acquisition of land could not be criticized on grounds of fairness as long as the Lockean proviso was satisfied.

Locke acknowledged that disparities did result from inheritance but placed the blame for the poverty of successive generations on the bad choices of their ancestors. If the initial acquisition of property rights were just (and Locke argued that they were since they sprang from the exercise of man's liberty to exercise his property in himself), and if the transfer of land was just (by contract or inheritance — the exercise of freedom to dispose of one's justly acquired assets), the state could not justly interfere with the existing distribution.

John Locke's theories about the relationship between the individual and the state dominated American political, social, and legal philosophy in the eighteenth century. They inspired the Declaration of Independence and were embodied in the federal Constitution and the constitutions of the states.

Locke's theories not only emphasized the origin of property rights in the exercise of liberty; they also had a strongly utilitarian apology for property in their explanation of social harmony in the beneficial use of resources.

There has always been a close association in American theory and practice between the personality theory of property and beneficial-use theories. Beneficial-use theories emphasize the harmonious and personal interaction between man and natural resources. "Squatters' rights" were recognized on the American frontier. If a man had cleared, settled, and occupied a parcel of land, he had first right to file a claim on it, and anyone else who wanted to claim it would have to buy out the squatter's share.

At the same time that the American courts recognized and protected property rights that had been established by beneficial use, courts and legislatures in the nineteenth century felt few qualms about allocating use rights to occupied and patented land if they expected that an increase in social benefits would arise from alternative land use. Railroad and canal companies were given liberal use of the power of eminent domain for the acquisition of right-of-ways with minimal compensation or legal protections for property owners in their path.

The prevailing philosophy associated with the "gospel of progress" seemed to be that an individual's personally-established property right to use land did not allow him to preclude its use by a private, profit-seeking railroad or canal company that (it was assumed) would be benefiting the general welfare. The gospel of progress did not allow the use of property rights to hinder development even if those property rights theoretically had their moral basis in the exercise of man's natural liberty to acquire property for his own beneficial use.

The Homestead Act of 1862 was a classic example of the embodiment of personality and beneficial-use theories as a basis for property rights. Claimants under the Homestead Act not only had to build a house on their land and farm it but they had to personally live on the land for at least half the year for five years before their property rights became absolute and transferable.

The beneficial-use aspect of the personality theory of property rights is also illustrated by the conditional character of property rights in practice in

American history. Adverse possession of land for seven years allows the occupier of the land to file for title. During the Great Depression, homes and farms being sold by the mortgagors after foreclosure found no potential purchasers. Community sentiment about the wrongness of the foreclosure of the previous owner-occupants was so high that potential purchasers were intimidated.

One of the best examples of the differing philosophic bases of property rights in the United States can be seen in the development of laws pertaining to the use of water.[4] The water laws that were taken to the colonies from England were based on the common-law system of riparian rights. Common-law riparian rights were *not* based on the temporal priority of claims and were an integral part of a complex and interdependent set of negotiated rules regarding complementary and conflicting uses of the land to which the riparian rights attached. England was a wet country, and the uses of water were nonconsumptive—there was no irrigation, water used to drive mills was returned to the same watercourse without loss of quality or quantity.

In the arid American West, water was needed for consumptive purposes—particularly irrigation and mining. It was often carried long distances, far from its original hydrologic basin for municipal water systems. It was not returned to its original watercourse undiminished in quantity or quality. It was appropriated for use by one person to the exclusion of others. Because the appropriation of water was only possible by costly and extensive capital investments, it was necessary to give some certainty to the continuing availability of water in order to justify the investments.

Appropriative water rights were established by the temporal order of diversion of water to beneficial use. They were separate and apart from property rights in land. They were not threatened by conflicting claims as long as the original appropriator continued to use the water for the same purposes, in the same seasonal pattern, and in the same quantity as the original filing. Appropriative rights became less secure and were open to challenge if they were not used or if they were used for a different purpose or if they were transferred to another party.

The philosophic basis of appropriative water rights was their *personal* creation by the appropriator of water in diverting it from its natural state to his own beneficial uses. This exercise of his personal liberty did not conflict with anyone else's liberty as long as there were alternatives open to others to go elsewhere in the sparsely settled American West.

Personality theories seem to lend themselves to philosophical systems in which some values are absolute. Marx's theory of property rights could be interpreted as a personality theory. Marx pointed out that labor was the *source* of all value and therefore laborers should receive the value of what they produced. Marx claimed that the operation of labor markets in a capitalist system were structured to prevent this from happening. Therefore the capitalist system should be replaced to allow a system of social organization that would ensure that labor did receive the value of its creation.

Some of the most interesting historical parts of *Das Kapital* describe the process by which the medieval peasantry were driven from their lands by the various Enclosure Acts that deprived them of their traditional use rights to land.[5] Marx argued that this dispossession was a necessary precondition to the development of capitalist labor markets since workers could not be exploited (paid less than the value of their labor) as long as peasants had the option of working their own land and receiving the full value of what they produced. Historical explanations of American social history in the nineteenth century such as the frontier theory of Frederick Jackson Turner explained the relative absence of radical and socialist movements in the United States by the availability of free land for settlement on the frontier that acted as a "safety valve" for social discontent and a guarantee of higher wages.

Ironically the personality theory of the origin of property rights in labor serves as a philosophic basis for both communism and capitalism. John Locke's origin of the theory has already been noted. Adam Smith, like Karl Marx, found the moral justification of his system in the labor theory of value and noted that markets served to guarantee that men would receive the value of what they had produced.

Currently, one of the important philosophic arguments against the modification of existing property rights comes from Libertarian philosophers of whom Robert Nozick is an articulate and persuasive spokesman.[6] Nozick's arguments are a sophisticated version of the personalist theory of the basis of property rights.

Nozick begins his treatise by declaring, "Individuals have rights and there are things no person or group may do to them (without violating their rights)." Nozick's argument posits that individuals' property rights, in our society, arise from the exercise of their own personal powers in the creation and exchange of personal services. He argues that it is therefore immoral for the government to interfere with distributions of rights that have originated in the exercise of men's personal powers and their modification and transfer by freely conducted exchange and bargaining. Nozick calls his theory a theory of "entitlement"; people are entitled to hold what they have acquired by legitimate processes of creation and transfer.

A personalist theory with a different emphasis is advanced by a contemporary legal philosopher, Charles A. Reich.[7] Reich notes that our society has traditionally attempted to nourish and protect the individual by vesting in him property rights to the use of physical assets that would afford him economic independence from the state. He then notes that economic independence and security in a modern industrial society are dependent to a large degree on income from employment, ownership of financial assets, and claims to transfer incomes from social security, welfare, unemployment compensation, aid to dependent children, and so on.

Reich argues for the establishment of property rights for individuals in a variety of transfer payments that may *not* have had their origins in labor and saving but that nevertheless are crucial to maintaining the independence of the individual against the state. Reich's insight and argument, of course, are not new. John Locke made the same argument for private property in the seventeenth century as the only way to assure the freedom of the individual and his independence from the state and other persons.

What implications do personalist theories of property have for the definition, distribution, and form of property rights as they are modified by shifts in the structure of land-use control mechanisms? The practical implications are probably fairly limited. The problems usually at issue in land-use control controversy are conflicting *uses* of resources where the absence or contradictory character of personal claims is the problem. Under a personalist theory the property right to use land in a manner that has been established by long-standing agricultural use scarcely implies the property right to use the same land for a factory *if* the use of the land for a factory imposes costs on neighboring landowners. Nor, conversely, are the rights of the neighboring landowners to the positive benefits conferred by an adjacent farm the type of property rights that are supposedly established by the type of personal action that justifies their protection under a personalist theory of property rights. A person's right to breathe clean air or to disperse pollutants into the air is not established by some past or present personal act, integral to the safeguarding of an individual's integrity in terms of personalist theory.

There is a very important distinction that does arise from personalist theories of property relative to the relationship between persons in their conflicting interests relative to the use of physical assets. That distinction relates to the role of the state as the regulator of rights established by individual action as opposed to the state as the originator of those rights.

This is a concept and a distinction with a long intellectual history. In Roman and medieval law it was the distinction between the sovereign as *dominium* and *imperium* — the distinction between the sovereign as master and as judge.[8]

In both Roman and medieval societies, the use of land and the control of slaves or serfs was a privilege conferred on certain men in return for civil or military obligations. The control of land or slaves depended on military conquest and occupation. The sovereign was the de facto source of the control of assets and any income that accrued to the person in whom control had been vested. In the absence of capital embodied in agricultural improvement or equipment, the ability of an individual to wrest any surplus from agricultural settlements over and above the subsistence of the slaves or serfs who worked them was assumed to be possible only by the physical exploitation that the sovereign would enforce.

In addition to the enforcement of control of land or slaves, Roman and medieval systems of organization had to regulate the relationships between citizens or freemen as a part of their role as regulator or *imperium*. This function was accomplished by the royal courts in the Middle Ages. A continuing struggle between the feudal nobility and the king (which began in England in 1216 with the Magna Carta and ended in 1660 with a parliamentary act assented to by the king that exchanged his right to levy feudal dues on land for the right to impose taxes on alcoholic beverages) was over the power of the sovereign arbitrarily to control the conditions of land use. The sovereign claimed that the right to control all land use arose from original conquest and occupation—that all land was part of the royal (French *real*) estate. The nobles argued that they (or their ancestors) had participated in the conquest, that the king was only *primus inter pares* (first among equals) and served only as a regulator or judge of disputes among subjects. The distinction between the role of the sovereign as *dominium* and *imperium* has been a continuing matter of controversy in political theory.

One important emphasis of personality theories of property is to focus attention on the role of individuals in the creation of contractual relationships that are enforced as property rights by the sovereign in its function as *imperium* or regulator of conflicts to preserve and enhance domestic tranquility. The sovereign protects and enforces the rights established between persons on a voluntary and negotiated basis when those rights have been established by procedures that are consensually considered to be appropriate and equitable.

John Locke's metaphor about man's establishing property in land by "mixing his labor with it" and Robert Nozick's arguments about Wilt Chamberlain's being *entitled* to hold the income that arises from audiences voluntarily paying to see him exercise his personal skills in playing basketball equally call attention to procedures for entitlement.[9] People have rights to assets acquired or appropriated by personal actions that other members of society regard as acceptable because there is not force and coercion of others entailed or implied by their actions. To use a modern description of the establishment of property rights, the process is "Pareto-optimal"—at least one party is better off as a result of the entitlement and no parties are worse off.

There is an important implication of this interpretation of personality theories as factual descriptions of negotiated processes; persons really do have to have successfully negotiated multilaterally voluntary agreements with all parties affected by resource use when property rights are defined. In practical terms, the impossibility of doing this could be interpreted as leading to the legislature and the courts, as the agents of all interested parties, modifying the terms of agreements.

Let me illustrate this principle with a specific example: the costs of air pollution were low relative to the costs of pollution control in the past so citizens had implicit property rights in the use of the air as a pollution disperser. The increase in urban densities and polluting technology changed the relative cost relationships, and various governments have been altering property rights as a consequence of changes in the implicitly negotiated property-rights agreements between citizens about the use of the air that is viewed as a common-property asset.

Another example of this principle might be illustrated by the refusal of a planning authority to allow the owner of agricultural land to develop it for industrial purposes. Society is assumed to have originally recognized the specific property claims of individuals to the agricultural use of the land because there were no uncompensated costs (or withdrawal of benefits) from others entailed in this recognition. Over the course of time, however, the redistribution of benefits that may be effected by the more intensive development of land does lead to conflicts that the planning authority does not allow to occur without some process of accommodation to the affected parties. In variance or rezoning proceedings, an important element in the administrative or judicial process is always the allowance for representations or protests by those affected by changes in land use. This could be explained as the allowance for the voluntary accommodation required by personalist theories of property rights.

As a summary comment on personality theories of property, it should be noted that they make an important contribution to an understanding of the "personal creation" characteristic of property rights. Where they fail as a useful basis for distinguishing between conflicting claims over resource use is in their failure to give an accurate and realistic description of the tentative, changing, and incomplete character of the negotiated relationships between people over their mutual privileges and forbearances. It is not very useful for one man to claim that he has a right to do as he will with the forest planted and nurtured by his ancestors if his removal of it were to destabilize a hillside, thus eroding his neighbor's land that had equally been cultivated from time immemorial by his ancestors (or acquired by the expenditure of income that originated in the sale of labor services).

While personalist theories call attention to the importance of individuals in creating rights, they ironically fail to carry out their own insight by making the definition of property rights an ongoing *process* of interaction.

Social-Contract Theories of Property

A second major category of philosophical theories about the origin and equity of property rights can be designated as "social-contract" or "utilitarian" theories. The distinguishing feature of these theories is that they call attention to the social creation (as opposed to personal creation) of property relationships, which increases the sum total of societal utility (benefit, good, welfare, and so on). These theories are of more ancient vintage than the individualist personality theories. Aristotle devotes a substantial portion of his *Politics* to exploring the alternative ways in which property rights might be structured to increase the harmony and prosperity of the state. In the Middle Ages the theory of the divine right of kings to structure property relationships as they saw fit was opposed by another theory that explained the arrangements governing land use as arising from the "custom of the manor" (*consuetudo manorii*).

Utilitarian theories emphasize the practical benefits from conferring rights to resource use on individuals to give them an incentive for their efficient use of resources and to reduce the costs of conflict. I have argued elsewhere that John Locke was really a precursor of the utilitarian tradition although he found it more persuasive to couch his arguments in the "natural rights" terminology of his age.[10] As noted previously, one could also interpret the beneficial-use doctrines of the American frontier as having a utilitarian, social-contractarian bent.

The important philosophic characteristic of utilitarian or incentive theories of property is that the moral or ethical precept upon which the systems are based is social rather than individual. The utilitarian postulate, for example, that social relationships *ought* to be structured to produce "the greatest good for the greatest number" means that the state would be taking appropriate action in the restructuring of property rights if it took them from one person whose utility (welfare, benefit, good) from them was less than the person(s) to whom they were transferred. Thus, to take an example from conflicts over land use, a utilitarian would find it entirely appropriate for a planning authority to transfer a water right from a lower value to higher value use by condemnation proceedings.

One of the most important reasons for regarding the social-utilitarian theory of property rights as the dominant American tradition has been the Supreme Court's interpretation of the Fifth and Fourteenth Amendments to the Constitution that prohibit the federal government or the states from "taking" private property without due process or just compensation. The Supreme Court has been loath to treat regulation (as opposed to physical dispossession) of property as a "taking" but has rather found regulation that affects the value of property to be an appropriate use of the police power (*imperium*) in the regulation of conflicts. The Supreme Court has found it legitimate for legislative bodies to redistribute and redefine property rights as long as it was done with procedural due process. The right of the legislature to attempt to secure the greatest good for the greatest number by the legislative process has been upheld.[11]

Utilitarian theories of property do not need to guarantee individual rights to any particular distribution of property. They require only that governmental actions to redistribute these property rights will not be so arbitrary as to undermine man's incentives to manage resources wisely.[12]

While the contemporary philosopher, John Rawls, specifically eschews utilitarian principles as a basis for social organization, his views on the appropriate basis for social organization belong in what could be categorized as social-contract theories.[13] Rawls argues that the moral basis of social arrangements depends upon the principles that rational men would agree on in a state of ignorance about their actual relative position in society. Rawls posits that what they would agree on would be equal liberty and a "difference principle" for income distribution. The difference principle would guarantee every member of society the maximum-minimum ("maximin") income possible from any set of resources and social and technological organization. Differences in income would be admissible only to the extent that they increased the *maximin* available to the least advantaged members of society.

A major criticism of utilitarianism has been that it provides no guarantee for the individual when his interests conflict with those of a majority. Rawls incorporates "a theory of justice" (the title of his book) into socially created arrangements to safeguard the individual against the overweening claims of the majority. The implication of Rawls's position for the protection of individual interests in land-use-control conflicts is that Rawls would enquire into the distributional consequences of existing patterns and changes in patterns of property rights in the evaluation of changes while utilitarians would be inclined to look only at the total social-welfare implications.

Social-contract theories of property rights pave the way for legislative activism in the redefinition of rights to resource use. They lack the absolute basis to entitlement to particular definitions and distributions of property rights that the personalist theories claim to possess. However, we have noted that the absolute-entitlement claims tend to be limited in their application to the types of conflict over resource use that are likely to arise in a complex interdependent society.

The strength and attractiveness of utilitarian theories is their attempt to order property relationships in a way that will maximize a society's collective utility with that maximization being represented as the revealed preferences of individuals in market transactions. Their weakness lies in their lack of protection for individual interests (an omission addressed by Rawls) and their neglect of the income-distribution consequences of assuming that individual utilities can be compared on the basis of market prices.

Psychological Theories of Property

A third set of philosophic theories about property rights could be categorized as psychological. They could also be referred to as empirical or social-
scientific theories as they tend to be based on the empirical observations of
anthropologists, historians, sociologists, and other social observers.

These psychological theories are based on man's observed attempts to
avoid or minimize uncertainty or insecurity. This type of theorizing or
generalizing about property rights tends to avoid equity judgments about
property rights but emphasizes the importance of recognized stability of
property relationships to minimize transactions costs and uncertainty.

Much of the modern property rights theorizing in economics seems to
be some mixture of this approach with a normative element emphasizing the
Pareto-optimal elements to be found in the personalist, individualist, and
social-contractarian approaches to property rights.[14] Milton Friedman,
Nobel Laureate in Economics and positivist observer of man's economic
behavior based on rational expectations, has written, "the existence of a
well specified and generally accepted definition of property is far more important than just what the definition is."[15] Friedman's approach to property
rights is to regard them as a means by which men reduce uncertainty, transactions, and enforcement costs.

Aristotle, our first positivist social scientist, could probably be cited as
a precursor of this approach. However, its first modern exposition in the
western intellectual tradition is to be found in the writings of David Hume.
As contrasted to Locke, Hume found the origins and evolution of social
organization stemming from affection and habit rather than rational, contractarian, and self-conscious creation of social arrangements. One might
almost class Hume's theories about the origins and evolution of social
organization as being a precursor of functionalist social Darwinian theories
based on the survival of forms and types of relationships suited to the
changing environment.

Hume theorized that men came to perceive the advantages of cooperation through experience and, concurrently, realized that the stability of
possession was dependent on mutual forbearance about persons' claims to
the use of resources. Property, for Hume, has its origin in the recognition of
the advantages of stability. As society develops and changes the rule-
making about property rights, it has to provide for stability of possession
and reduction of conflict about property claims to new or previously
unclaimed resources.

Like the social contractarians' emphasis on rational creation of property rights, the psychological theories of property depend on *agreements*
between members of society about the terms and conditions of resource use
to explain the nature of property rights. The social contractarian approach
emphasizes conscious and rational creation of property rights, while the
psychological theories emphasize recognition of property rights that arise

from random human behavior and endure because of their suitability in a process of nonteleological natural selection.

The great practical difference between the two approaches, for our purposes, is the difference between them with respect to the importance of the stability of property rules and the stability of expectations about property rules. Social contractarians would find no problem with continual changes in the rules and would argue that men will adapt their expectations to take uncertainty into account.

Psychological theories, on the other hand, would argue that insecurity about the future form of property rights, or expectations that they would be changed, would have a very deleterious effect on social arrangements and contribute to social disintegration by weakening the force of habit. Some psychological theorists would argue that in the absence of a substantial measure of certainty that existing property relationships will be maintained, long-term investment and productivity-increasing behavior will be substantially reduced.

What is important about the psychological theories is not that all redistributions or redefinitions of property rights be avoided but that uncertainty and, particularly, *arbitrary* redistribution (as between types or classes of persons or between individuals), be avoided. The importance of this principle has been enshrined in the U.S. Constitution in the requirement that all citizens will be afforded "equal protection" under the law with Congress specifically prohibited from passing bills of attainder (legislation directed at a specific person) or ex post facto laws.

The question might be asked about the importance of governmental nonintervention with respect to property rights when the changes wrought by economic and technological forces are constantly changing the costs and benefits associated with asset use. Why should the uncertainties created by state intervention be different from the uncertainties introduced by other members of society? An answer to this question would be made by psychological theorists in terms of limiting the areas of conflict between individuals by precluding struggles for political power to change asset distributions and limiting those struggles to nongovernmental disputes. The answer, while reasonable, is hardly persuasive.

Conclusions and Implications

What implications for the equity issue, in land-use planning, do the three categories of theories about property rights have? Three conclusions can be drawn from these theories that are relevant criteria for the evaluation of principles controlling land and resource use.

A first principle of environmental-control mechanisms and land-use planning should be the stability of possession of existing-use rights. In other words, land-use rules should not be promulgated that require an owner to change the present use of land. In agricultural or silvicultural use, for example, land should not have regulations applied to it that forbid the continuation of that use to, say, provide recreational opportunities or environmental amenities for the public.

This principle is based on the personalist and psychological theories of the origin and nature of property rights. People have invested themselves in existing patterns of land use, and those investments of personality cannot be violated without offense and violence to individuals. In addition, uncertainty about arbitrary state action to change existing patterns of property rights would be socially and psychologically disruptive and destabilizing.

It should be noted that the stability of possession principles advanced here is stability of possession of particular use rights. Nothing implied by this principle would give *new* rights to the owner of existing rights to use land or other natural resources. For example, property rights to use a particular plot of land for residential use cannot be implied, under the stability-of-possession rule, to give their holder the undisputed right to turn those residential rights into commercial or industrial rights to land use.

A second principle for land-use-control systems should be their recognition of the interdependence of costs and benefits and the matching of costs and benefits, insofar as possible. One of the important features of social-contractarian theories of property is their explicit recognition that man's behavior can be controlled contractually. This needs to be embodied in rules that fit the principle that "he who enjoys the benefit pays the cost."

The application of this principle might be illustrated by the enjoyment of a park by neighboring landowners. Maintaining the land as a park has a cost in terms of alternative uses foregone as well as operating costs. If the land is maintained as a park by public authority, part of the cost may be recovered by the public authority through the imposition of ad valorem taxes on the market value of the land that is increased in value by proximity to the park. A more important application of this principle will be seen in payment of use fees for the use of land for the provision of public goods and marginal-cost pricing for public utilities.

A third principle, drawn from all three theories about the nature of property rights, is that redistribution of property rights to the use of natural resources should not be undertaken primarily to redistribute income and wealth. Where redistribution of income does take place as a result of regulation, there should be compensation to maintain the status quo ante position of the parties affected adversely. This third principle should not imply, in any way, that it is inappropriate to redistribute income. However, the stability-of-possession principle emphasized by both the personalist and psychological theories of property, and the importance of the incentive theory in the social-contractarian theory of property, should alert us to the importance to the social framework of stability of possession to use of physical assets. Since there is a long-acknowledged legitimacy and expectation about the governmental imposition of taxes on income and expenditure, even for purposes of income redistribution, it could be argued that this is a preferable approach to income redistribution and that this important factor should be kept out of the conflicts that inevitably arise from changing property rights to resource use. This principle has its counterpart in welfare economics where redistributions of rights to assets that increase total utility but alter distribution should be accompanied by compensation.[16]

As Blackstone noted, "there is no foundation in nature or in natural law, why a set of words upon parchment should convey the dominion of land." Nevertheless, there are strong foundations in human nature and beliefs about equity that need to inform modification of existing laws and practices that control the use of land and the physical environment of our human society.[17]

Notes

1. William Blackstone, *Commentaries on the Law of England* (Philadelphia: Robert Bell, 1771), book II, p. 2.

2. R.H. Coase, "The Problem of Social Cost," *Journal of Law and Economics* 3 (October 1960).

3. John Locke, *Second Treatise on Civil Government* (London: 1690). For a modern edition, see Peter Laslett, *Two Treatises of Government* (Cambridge: Cambridge University Press, 1960).

4. For a more extensive discussion, see Gordon C. Bjork, "Property, Scarcity, and Economic Rent: Some Applications to Water Rights," in *Economics of Natural Resource Development in the West*, Human Resources and Natural Resources Committee of the Western Agricultural Economics Research Council (Fort Collins, Col.: 1974).

5. Karl Marx, *Capital* (New York: The Modern Library, 1906), chap. 27.

6. Robert Nozick, *Anarchy, State and Utopia* (New York: Basic Books, 1974).

7. Charles A. Reich, *inter alia*, "The Law of the Planned Society," *Yale Law Journal* 75 (no. 8) (1966); "The New Property," *The Public Interest* 3 (1966); *The Greening of America* (New York: Random House, 1970).

8. See Roscoe Pound, *An Introduction to the Philosophy of Law* (New Haven, Conn.: Yale University Press, 1954), chap. on "Property."

9. Nozick, *Anarchy, State and Utopia*, chap. 7.

10. G.C. Bjork, *Private Enterprise and Public Interest: The Development of American Capitalism* (Englewood Cliffs, N.J.: Prentice-Hall, 1969), chap. 3, 4, 5.

11. F. Bosselman, D. Callies, and J. Banta, *The Taking Issue* (Washington, D.C.: Council on Environmental Quality, 1973).

12. For a classical discussion of utilitarian views on property, see John Stuart Mill, *Principles of Political Economy* (London: John Parker, 1848), book II, chap. 1, sec. 3.

13. John Rawls, *A Theory of Justice* (Cambridge, Mass.: Belknap Press of Harvard University Press, 1971).

14. A review of the literature may be found in E. Furobotn and S. Pejovich, "Property Rights and Economic Theory: A Survey of Recent Literature," *Journal of Economic Literature* 10 (no. 4) (December 1972).

15. Milton Friedman, *Capitalism and Freedom* (Chicago: University of Chicago Press, 1962), p. 27.

16. See, for example, I.M.D. Little, *A Critique of Welfare Economics* (Oxford: Clarendon Press, 1950), chap. 1 and 4.

17. A classic essay on the philosophic bases of the law with respect to property rights may be found in Frank I. Michelman, "Property, Utility, and Fairness: Comments on the Ethical Foundations of Just Compensation Law," *Harvard Law Review* 80 (April 1967), pp. 1165-1258.

5

The American Legal Framework for Land-Use Control

Private property in land has been a fundamental premise of the American republic since its inception two centuries ago. Thomas Jefferson did not state in the Declaration of Independence as the English philosopher John Locke had done a century earlier, that men had inalienable rights to "life, liberty, and property" — only to "life, liberty, and the pursuit of happiness." Yet many Americans believe that private property in land and the liberty to use it as they see fit are as important as, and indistinguishable from, personal liberty.

Over the last two centuries of American history, the strongly held views about the relationship between personal liberty and the use of land and other natural resources have created fundamental tensions for American legislatures and the courts in the regulation and control of land use.

The preceding chapters have explored the inevitability of conflict over land use between citizens, and the economic consequences and the philosophic bases of the rules that structure property rights in the use of land. This chapter will explore the way in which conflicts have been resolved and principles applied in the development of the American economic and legal framework for the control of land use.

The constitutional powers of the state and federal governments to regulate the use of labor, capital, and land are now well established. When state and federal governments in the nineteenth century first asserted control over railway rates or sanitary conditions in packing houses or maximum hours and working conditions for women and children, objections were taken all the way to the Supreme Court on the grounds that those attempts to regulate economic activity were an unconstitutional interference with personal liberty and private property. The decisions that established the constitutionality, and the theoretical and practical bases for the regulation of land use, were passed down by the Supreme Court in the *Pennsylvania Coal* v. *Mahon*, and *Euclid* v. *Ambler*[1] cases in the 1920s.

In those cases the court ruled that the state regulation of the use of land by prohibitions on certain uses or local control by zoning sometimes did and sometimes did not represent an unconstitutional regulation or "taking" of private property in land without due process and just compensation.

The powers of state and local government to regulate land use were affirmed to be an appropriate exercise of the police power to protect public health and safety. Even so, the right of the individual American citizen or corporation to pursue economic self-interest in the use of land, free from the arbitrary exercise of power by the state, was held to be a constitutionally protected right of the American people that the court would protect from abuse by local government. Even though these decisions are now a half-century behind us, and numerous other decisions in state and federal courts have elaborated and extended the principles decided in these cases, this chapter will consider them at length because they identify the principles upon which the American social framework for the control of conflicts over land use is premised.

How is the liberty to use land, guaranteed by property rights, reconciled with the constraints on liberty to use land imposed by zoning and other limitations on land use? Property rights protect one's land from the actions of others. The use of land, reciprocally, is restricted in order to prevent certain uses that might harm the interests of others. Property rights in one's own land are balanced with the obligation to use it in ways that will respect the property rights of others in their safety, health, welfare, and the enjoyment of their assets.

Zoning is the land-use-control device in general use that extends, limits, and defines land use, that secures the conferral of valuable environmental amenities, and that prevents the imposition of undesirable neighborhood effects. Zoning laws prohibit one party from using his property in certain ways that will be deleterious to the interests of others. Zoning laws specify the permitted uses of land within a designated geographic area.

Zoning laws might be viewed partly as a codification and specification of the laws of nuisance. Certain uses of land constitute a "nuisance" to others and are, consequently, proscribed. Zoning limits the allowable uses of property. It is an administrative means of controlling the uses of property that would otherwise result from the exchange and use of property rights in land in response to market forces.

Restrictions on the use of land, like private property in land, are a necessary feature of social organization in any society in which there is a shortage of land. Like property rules, zoning rules perform an allocative and distributive function. But instead of providing incentives for the landowner to allocate his land to a use that would be most profitable for him, they preclude him from doing so because of the effects his land use might have on the use and enjoyment by others of their property.

Zoning laws are redistributive in their effects. Zoning and other forms of land-use restriction both confer benefits and restrict the realization of gains (or even inflict costs) on land in private ownership. Reclassification of land for industrial use will substantially increase its market value (in most instances). A variance for a gas station in a residential neighborhood may benefit the owner of the land where it is located and injure the owners of neighboring properties. The gains for the owner of the land on which the gas station is located may be substantially less than the losses for the adjoining property owners.

The redistributional effects of zoning occur because the ownership of land is dispersed randomly over the area in which land is zoned from lower to higher intensity uses. Some landowners benefit and some lose from zoning decisions. What principles justify the use of political power for this random redistribution of wealth? What principles presently control the use of this power? What principles should control the use of this power in the future?

Zoning has been in common use in municipalities in the United States for almost a century. Zoning laws are passed in order to prevent the adverse spillover effects that would occur to the owner of one piece of property when an adjoining property is used for a more intensive use. They are also used to force the provision of favorable spillover effects from property owners to adjoining property owners.

The owner of a suburban home would not like to have a gas station located next door because the noise and smells that are the necessary accompaniment to a gas station would lessen the enjoyment and, hence, the market value of his home. While he could bring a legal action under the law of nuisance to prevent the intrusions on his enjoyment of his property, or negotiate to prevent the noxious use by compensation, zoning laws make simple and less costly the maintenance of environmental amenity that is a desirable characteristic of residential sites. They also define the nature of environmental amenities that are to be recognized and protected in towns.

An integral part of zoning regulations is a variety of specifications as to the way in which land can be used in connection with the purpose for which it is zoned. Minimum lot-size requirements specify the smallest size of lot that may be used for residential purposes. Density requirements specify the maximum and minimum heights and setbacks from property lines. Building codes specify acceptable materials and construction standards. In areas where public water and sewer systems are not available, the standards for private wells and septic drainage fields are specified.

All these requirements about the use that the owner of property may make of his land are legislated by local governments under the police power provisions of federal and state constitutions that make the protection of public health and safety a local government responsibility. The rationale for including these regulations as part of the police power to protect public health and safety is the principle that the owner of a residential site does *not* have the right to build a house in such a way that it might endanger the health or safety of his visitors, himself, or future purchasers of the property. The owner of a parcel of land does not have the right to use it for nonresidential uses in a neighborhood that is zoned for residential use only for the reason that this would impose adverse spillover effects—detrimental to public health and safety—on his neighbors.

It is important to note that the restrictions placed on land use by zoning arise from the same sort of conflicts that private property evolved to deal with, but with an important difference; they attempt to prohibit the imposition of costs and require the conferral of benefits on others—rather than internalizing them. They extend, limit, specify, and generalize use rights.

It will be recalled from chapter 3 that the argument for the conversion of land from common ownership to individual ownership was that such conversion would "internalize externalities." The costs of grazing the additional animal on the common might be large for all the other users of the common, but the individual's share of these costs might be small in relation to the benefit for the individual user. The small, realized benefit for the individual was larger than his share of the common cost, even though these costs far exceeded his benefit. Thus the incentives for the individual were to go on imposing costs on others unless he could get *all* to agree to stop doing so and thus enjoy the gains. Because the transactions and enforcement costs of this solution were high, individual private property rights developed to allow the individual to internalize costs and benefits.

Mutual coercion, mutually agreed on, to stop the infliction of costs and require the conferral of benefits on others is the essence of zoning. It stops the infliction of costs and requires the bestowal of benefits by all members of a neighborhood on all the others and, thereby, in theory increases the total benefit available to each and every property owner. And this result is secured with low transaction and enforcement costs. Or so the argument goes.

Zoning is land-use designation. Land may be zoned for more or less intensive uses. Intensive use usually has the highest market value and imposes the most extensive costs on adjoining owners. Thus extractive, industrial, commercial, multifamily residential, single-family residence, and agricultural uses run the continuum from the most to the least intensive uses.

Land zoned for high-intensity use will usually have the highest value per acre in a community, while land zoned for low-intensity use will have the lowest value per acre. Values are also determined by scarcity. Thus in the zoning process, there is an incentive for landowners to try to get their own land zoned for highly intensive uses and the land of others zoned for lower intensity uses. If all the land in a community were zoned industrial, it would have less value than if only a small amount were. An additional consideration in the zoning process arises from the individual's incentive to try to have land originally zoned lower intensity rezoned to a higher intensity use because it will have a lower acquisition cost and because it may have some environmental amenities that are valuable to him.

This consideration is particularly important in residential use. A would-be homeowner may benefit from the lower cost per acre and the openspace amenities of agricultural or open land if he can build on it rather than on land zoned residential. A factory owner or merchant may have similar incentives in terms of land costs (although locational characteristics such as access to freeways or rail lines may be of more importance to this decision).

Zoning decisions are inevitably made in the midst of economic conflicts of interest. Each landowner has an interest in getting his own land zoned for higher intensity uses and the land of others zoned for lower intensity uses. These conflicts have historically been partially mitigated by "spot zoning," by the use of variances—exceptions from the general rule—and the allowance for continuation of nonconforming uses that were in existence when zoning regulations were made.

The political acceptability of the zoning process has been understandable partially because the gainers from intensive zoning were always strong supporters while the losses of those whose property was zoned for lower intensity uses were losers only in the sense that they did not realize potential gains. And then many potential losers who complained loudly enough were granted variances or spot zoning to allow their realization of higher value uses for their properties over the objections of their neighbors and others whose incentives for opposing variance or spot zoning were not nearly so strong individually as were the incentives of those who sought them.

Zoning and other regulations of the use of property limit the costs that can be imposed by one member of society on another by general prohibitions on certain activities. It would also be possible for individual members of a society to deal with the costs and benefits by contractual agreement. Or it would be possible for individuals, adversely affected by a neighbor's use of land, to seek injunctive relief.

Why has zoning been the most popular way in which to deal with the problem of external costs and benefits? The traditional argument for zoning has been its supposedly lower transaction costs. It is, allegedly, less costly for the residents of a municipality to pass a zoning ordinance relegating various types of industrial, commercial, and residential land uses to separate zones within the municipality than to draw up a multilateral set of covenants and agreements among themselves to circumscribe and specify all the uses to which specific lands could be put.[2]

It is also presumably less costly for members of a community to zone than to bring legal actions under the law of nuisances whenever undesirable activities by an individual on his land lessen the use and enjoyment of his neighbor's. Zoning also defines the nature of nuisance and could be seen as a means of increasing certainty (and thereby lowering costs) of bringing actions to remedy conflicting land uses.

Lower transactions costs are only part of the explanation for the popularity of zoning. Another important reason for the use of zoning, rather than private agreements or injunctive relief, is that zoning will bring a different distribution of costs and benefits to landowners than the other two methods of reconciling conflicting land use.

Let us illustrate this by the use of an example. Suppose that a gas station is proposed in a residential neighborhood. The gas station operator would be willing to pay several times as much for the use of a corner lot as would any homeowner. The adjacent property owners, however, estimate that the location of the gas station in the neighborhood will substantially lessen the enjoyment of their residential amenities and the value of their properties. They therefore offer to compensate the owner of the land on which the proposed gas station is to be built to incorporate an exclusion of any but residential use into the provisions governing use of the parcel of land in question.

The compensation of the property owner of the land where the gas station was to be located by the other landowners results in a partial redistribution of wealth. The residential owners have to take explicit account of the value they receive from *not* having a gas station next to them by compensating the owner of the adjacent property for not using it for that purpose. He is as well off with the compensation from the adjoining landowners as he would be if he had leased or sold the land for the operation of the gas station; the amount of compensation he would demand for not siting a gas station would, presumably, not be less than he would have received for the use of the site for a gas station.

The residential owners are presumably better off than they would have been if the gas station had been built, or otherwise they would not have been willing to pay the compensation. In the absence of a zoning law, the distribution of wealth between the owner of the potential gas station site and the other landowners would be different than if zoning laws prohibited the gas station without the necessity of negotiated compensation.

Passing a zoning law restricting the use of land allows the owners of land used for less intensive uses to avoid the payment of compensation to the owners of land suitable for more intensive uses. It deprives the owners of land that could be more intensively used of the higher returns they could have received for those uses, or the compensation they could have demanded for forgoing those uses. It could also result in a situation in which the owner and society were deprived of a valuable land use and there were no or less offsetting benefits to adjacent landowners.

The redistribution of wealth by zoning, however, is not a straightforward matter. If the land had not been zoned exclusively for residential purposes and was used for a variety of industrial, commercial, and residential purposes, all the land might have had less value for residential use and the owners might not have been willing to pay compensation to the owner of the service station site not to locate a service station on the site. Also if land were not zoned, the availability of a variety of different sites might have made any potential service station operator less willing to pay a premium for a particular site because of the availability of alternative service station sites. Zoning is the mechanism that creates some of the values available for redistribution as well as redistributing them.

Governmental activity in zoning may be viewed positively as collective action by the members of a society to reduce transactions and enforcement costs and to create a social framework that enhances the welfare of all members of the society. It is the creation of values by zoning for all property owners within a zone or the zoned community that makes it an appropriate use of the police power. The benefits of zoning are reciprocal for all the landowners in an area zoned for a particular use. In the absence of zoning, the value of all the land within the zone would be less than when zoned because of the diminution of values caused by incompatible uses.

Zoning is mutual coercion, mutually agreed on by the property owners in a particular community, to prevent any one of them from following the maximization of his own wealth in a way that would decrease the wealth of other property owners by *more* than the increase in his wealth. It has the same logic as the creation of property rights for exclusive use to internalize the costs and benefits. Zoning is legitimated as a political activity because it is a net creator of value rather than a mere redistributor.

There is a parallel argument here with the use of the police power to proscribe robbery. Why should we employ a police force to proscribe robbery rather than allowing every potential victim to bribe potential robbers not to rob him? One argument might be the lower cost of hiring police than negotiating with potential robbers. The more important argument surely is that the total welfare of the community is increased by diverting human activity into wealth creation rather than the activities of threatening coercion in order to redistribute wealth. The moral argument for wealth creation and against mere wealth distribution is that the former benefits the whole community while the latter does not.

While the principles supporting the use of zoning, rather than individual contracts or injunctive relief under the law of nuisances, are fairly straightforward, their application and outcomes are not. The possibility that zoning *may* increase the welfare of all members of a community does not guarantee that a specific set of zoning regulations *will* accomplish this objective.

Suppose, for example, that a small electronics factory wanted to locate in a residential neighborhood because its highly skilled employees wanted to live in that neighborhood and walk to work. Because of the preferences of its employees, the factory owner would be willing to pay a very large premium over the market price for residential use for the land; in economic theory, this premium might represent the amount that the employees would forgo in pay rather than commute to a different site where the company would have to pay them higher wages to compensate them for the commute and to leave them as well off as they would have been walking to work.

Suppose further that the electronics factory imposed no objectionable effects on its neighbors. Suppose, in fact, that it was housed in a beautiful building in beautiful grounds that were used as a park by the neighborhood. The effect of the zoning regulation that zones the factory out of the neighborhood would be a substantial social loss—a measure of which was the site rent which the factory would have been willing to pay. The zoning may increase auto traffic with its attendant personal and social costs. (In this example, we are assuming that the factory imposed no negative side-effects on the other residents.) Zoning may be a blunt instrument that lessens as well as increases total property values in a community.

Zoning powers may be used in ways that could result in loss of benefits to individual landowners with no offsetting benefits to other landowners such as in the electronics factory example. They can also be used in a way that brings no reciprocal benefits to the owners of some property.

Individual citizens with grievances against zoning restrictions on the use of property can appeal to the courts against the use of zoning that is "unreasonable," or inappropriate to the public purposes for which it is a means, which deprives them of all reasonable uses, or which takes valuable uses of their property for public benefit with no reciprocal benefits to them without due process or compensation. An understanding of the principles that underlie the definition of appropriate use of zoning for the definition and specification of land-use rules must be sought in the law.

The legitimacy of zoning laws as an appropriate exercise of the police power was first affirmed and justified by the Supreme Court of the United States in *Euclid* v. *Ambler* in 1926. In this case, the Ambler Realty Company disputed the constitutionality of zoning laws passed by the incorporated village of Euclid, Ohio. The Euclid City Council zoned part of the property that the Ambler Realty Company had planned to develop for industrial purposes as residential use only. It is appropriate to quote from the decision of the court, affirming the constitutionality of zoning laws under the police powers, at length:

> Building zone laws are of modern origin. They began in this country about twenty-five years ago. Until recent years, urban life was comparatively simple; but with the great increase and concentration of population, problems have developed, and constantly are developing, which require, and will continue to require, additional restrictions in respect of the use and occupation of private lands in urban communities. Regulations, the wisdom, necessity and validity of which, as applied to existing conditions, are so apparent that they are now uniformly sustained, a century ago, or even half a century ago, probably would have been rejected as arbitrary and oppressive. Such regulations are sustained, under the complex conditions of our day, for reasons analogous to those which justify traffic regulations, . . .

> The ordinance now under review, and all similar laws and regulations, must find their justification in some aspect of the police power, asserted for the public welfare. The line which in this field separates the legitimate from the illegitimate assumption of power is not capable of precise delimitation. It varies with circumstances and conditions. A regulatory zoning ordinance, which would be clearly valid as applied to the great cities, might be clearly invalid as applied to rural communities. In resolving doubts, the maxim *sic utere tuo ut alienum non laedas*, which lies at the foundation of so much of

the common law of nuisances, ordinarily will furnish a fairly helpful clew. And the law of nuisances, likewise, may be consulted, not for the purposes of controlling, but for the helpful aid of its analogies in the process of ascertaining the scope of, the power. Thus the question whether the power exists to forbid the erection of a building of a particular kind or for a particular use, like the question whether a particular thing is a nuisance, is to be determined, not by an abstract consideration of the building or of the thing considered apart, but by considering it in connection with the circumstances and the locality . . . . A nuisance may be merely a right thing in the wrong place, like a pig in the parlor instead of the barnyard. If the validity of the legislative classification for zoning purposes be fairly debatable, the legislative judgment must be allowed to control . . . .

It is said that the village of Euclid is a mere suburb of the City of Cleveland; that the industrial development of that city has now reached and in some degree extended into the village and, in the obvious course of things, will soon absorb the entire area for industrial enterprises; that the effect of the ordinance is to divert this natural development elsewhere with the consequent loss of increased values to the owners of the lands within the village borders. But the village, though physically a suburb of Cleveland, is politically a separate municipality, with powers of its own and authority to govern itself as it sees fit within the limits of the organic law of its creation and the State and Federal Constitutions. Its governing authorities, presumably representing a majority of its inhabitants and voicing their will, have determined, not that industrial development shall cease at its boundaries, but that the course of such development shall proceed within definitely fixed lines. If it be a proper exercise of the police power to relegate industrial establishments to localities separated from residential sections, it is not easy to find a sufficient reason for denying the power because the effect of its exercise is to divert an industrial flow from the course which it would follow, to the injury of the residential public if left alone, to another course where such injury will be obviated. It is not meant by this, however, to exclude the possibility of cases where the general public interest would so far outweigh the interest of the municipality that the municipality would not be allowed to stand in the way.

The *Euclid* v. *Ambler* decision makes three important distinctions about the necessity and scope of zoning as a specification of the laws of property: (1) zoning is the necessary concomitant of the interdependence in land use that comes from urbanization; (2) zoning must be left to local authorities because the values defined and protected are a matter of taste and custom; and (3) the zoning laws of a particular community may conflict with the broader interests of the general public, in which case, the local community could be overruled. The court has always reserved the right to pass on the specifics of legislation that might not, in the judgment of the court, comprise a "reasonable use" of the police power. The court voided almost three decades ago zoning laws and private agreements designed to racially segregate neighborhoods. Since the *Brown* v. *Board of Education* decision in 1953, communities have been required to integrate school districts even when this required the bringing of children from one area to another because of de facto segregation. In two recent cases the Supreme Court has withheld the constitutionality of restrictions by the cities of Petaluma, California, and Boulder, Colorado, to limit their growth. It has also upheld the right of a suburb of Chicago to enforce zoning regulations limiting density that were alleged to have the effect of excluding low-income blacks. The Court ruled in the latter case that the municipality was engaged in a proper exercise of the police power as long as the *intent* to the legislation was not the exclusion of blacks. The power of a local community to regulate land use through zoning has far-reaching implications for social policy.

What the *Euclid* v. *Ambler* decision did not resolve (or even address) was the principles regarding equity and efficiency that are at issue in zoning decisions. The common-law rule cited (*sic utere tuo ut alienum non laedas*, "use your own property in a way that does not burden others") begs the question if property rights are not defined but in conflict. Should the owner of the gas station corner have the property right to use the land to satisfy the convenience needs of motorists to the detriment of neighboring owners? Or do the adjoining owners have the right to peace and quiet to the detriment of the motorists' convenience?

The continuing dilemma for city council, state legislature, and the courts in all laws that regulate the use of land is that the rules abridge the powers of the parties with conflicting uses to negotiate over the uses of land that will be the highest and best uses. This raises questions of both equity and efficiency. The courts need to address themselves to both issues in considering the operation of legislation controlling land use.

The landmark case of *Pennsylvania Coal Co.* v. *Mahon* (1922) illustrates the nature of judicial thinking on the equity and efficiency issues. In the case under consideration, the U.S. Supreme Court ruled that an act of the Pennsylvania legislature that prohibited the mining of coal in such a way as to cause subsidence on the property of others was an unconstitutional "taking" of the property of the coal company.

In the case at issue, the residential property of Mahon, threatened with subsidence by coal mining, had originally been sold to him by the coal company without the underground mineral rights and without liability for any subsidence that might occur through their exercise. Property rights had been limited and defined on the residential property by mutual prior agreement of the parties.

The law passed by the Pennsylvania legislature prohibited the coal company from mining in such a way that it would cause subsidence to the Mahon residence. In voiding the application of the Pennsylvania legislation in this instance, Justice Holmes noted:

> Government hardly could go on if to some extent values incident to property could not be diminished without paying for every such change in the general law. As long recognized, some values are enjoyed under an implied

limitation which must have its limits, or the contract and due process clauses (of the 5th and 14th Amendments to the Constitution of the U.S.) are gone. One fact for consideration in determining such limits is the extent of the diminution. When it reaches a certain magnitude, in most if not in all cases there must be an exercise of eminent domain and compensation to sustain the act. So the question depends upon the particular facts. The greatest weight is given to the judgment of the legislature, but it always is open to interested parties to contend that the legislature has gone beyond its constitutional power . . . .

The general rule at least is, that while property may be regulated to a certain extent, if regulation goes too far it will be recognized as a taking . . . . In general it is not plain that a man's misfortunes or necessities will justify shifting the damages to his neighbor's shoulders . . . . We are in danger of forgetting that a strong public desire to improve the public condition is not enough to warrant achieving the desire by a shorter cut than the constitutional way of paying for the change. As we already have said, this is a matter of degree—and therefore cannot be disposed of by general propositions . . . .

The opinion of the majority was that "too much" of the value of the Pennsylvania Coal Company's property in coal had been taken by restrictions on its mining methods and therefore that the legislation was an unconstitutional "taking."

It should be noted that the laws against subsidence did not obtain where the surface lands were owned by the coal company. It would have been open to the coal company to purchase the surface land on which subsidence would occur as a result of the coal-mining operation. This would have the effect of making the coal company (and the purchasers of coal) take into account the value of the damage done to the surface properties by the extraction of coal.

In a very interesting dissent to the case, Justice Brandeis argued that the operation of the law being tested in the case would force the company to do this:

Every restriction upon the use of property imposed in the exercise of the police power deprives the owner of some right theretofore enjoyed, and is, in that sense, an abridgment by the State of rights in property without making compensation. But restriction imposed to protect the public health, safety or morals from dangers threatened is not a taking. The restriction here in question is merely the prohibition of a noxious use. The property so restricted remains in the possession of its owner. The State does not appropriate it or make any use of it. The State merely prevents the owner from making a use which interfered with paramount rights of the public. Whenever the use prohibited ceases to be noxious, as it may because of further change in local or social conditions, the restriction will have to be removed and the owner will again be free to enjoy his property as heretofore.

The restriction upon the use of this property cannot, of course, be lawfully imposed, unless its purpose is to protect the public. But the purpose of a restriction does not cease to be public, because incidentally some private persons may thereby receive gratuitously valuable special benefits. Thus, owners of low buildings may obtain, through statutory restrictions upon the height of neighboring structures, benefits equivalent to an easement of light and air . . . .

Nor is a restriction imposed through exercise of the police power inappropriate as a means, merely because the same end might be effected through exercise of the power of eminent domain, or otherwise at public expense. Every restriction upon the height of buildings might be secured through acquiring by eminent domain the right of each owner to build above the limiting height; but it is settled that the State need not resort to that power . . . .

It is said that one fact for consideration in determining whether the limits of the police power have been exceeded is the extent of the resulting diminution in value; and that here the restriction destroys existing rights of property and contract. But values are relative. *If we are to consider the value of the coal kept in place by restriction, we should compare it with the value of all other parts of the land. That is, with the value not of the coal alone, but with the value of the whole property.* [Italics added.] The rights of an owner as against the public are not increased by dividing the interests in his property into surface and subsoil. The sum of the rights in the parts cannot be greater than the rights in the whole. The estate of an owner in land is grandiloquently described as extending *ab orco usque ad coelum.* But I suppose no one would contend that by selling his interest above one-hundred feet from the surface he could prevent the State from limiting, by the police power, the height of structures in a city. And why should a sale of underground rights bar the State's power . . . ."

The conclusion (that the right to curb the subsidence resulting from coal mining is an unwarranted exercise of police power) seems to rest upon the assumption that in order to justify such exercise of the police power there must be "an average reciprocity of advantage" as between the owner of the property restricted and the rest of the community; and that here such reciprocity is absent. *Reciprocity of advantage is an important consideration, and may even be essential, where the State's power is exercised for the purpose of conferring benefits upon the property of a neighborhood, as in drainage projects* [italics added] . . . . But where the police power is exercised, not to confer benefits upon property owners, but to protect the public from detriment and danger, there is, in my opinion, no room for considering reciprocity of advantage . . . . unless it be the advantage of living and doing business in a civilized community. The reciprocal advantage is given by the act to the coal operators.

At issue in this case are both matters of efficiency and equity. Justice Holmes has noted that if the surface owner of land, who has purchased it without protection against subsidence, wants to add that element to it, he must be prepared to compensate the owner for it and not have the state take it for him by a regulation that accomplishes it by a taking. Justice Brandeis has noted that the coal-mine owner should be forced to take into account the diminution of the value of surface land caused by mining. Pennsylvania Coal Company had already done this when they sold the land at a lower price with reservations.

It is my argument that the public interest is not the adjudication of property rights or police powers to distribute benefits to a specific party in a conflict. The public interest is to establish rules that will cause both to consider the costs imposed on the other in calculations so that the use of land that is made will be that with the highest net benefits — those benefits to be determined by the conflicting parties to land use through negotiation.

In terms of equity considerations, Justice Holmes noted that if a regulation confiscates too much of the value of one man's property for the benefit of the public at large, it will not be allowed. Justice Brandeis notes that reciprocity of advantage is important "when the State's power is exercised for the purpose of conferring benefits upon the property of a neighborhood . . . but where the police power is exercised, not to confer benefits upon property owners, but to protect the public from detriment and danger, there is . . . no room for considering reciprocity of advantage."

I would extend Brandeis's argument. Any use of assets that inflicts detriment or danger upon the public generally cannot be guaranteed the protection of private property and is subject to regulation under the police power. On the other hand, the police power may not be used to make a property owner provide benefits to the public without compensation. The problem here, as noted in chapter 3 is that it is arbitrary to distinguish between the withdrawal of a benefit and the infliction of a detriment. The provision of land stability may be considered a benefit (conferred at a cost in terms of lost coal) or the infliction of subsidence may be viewed as a detriment.

There are two inevitable problems involved in the use of legislation to make decisions about conflicting land use. The equity problem of deciding how much of the diminution in value is too much is readily apparent. The efficiency problem is not so apparent and is entangled with the use of the police power. What constitutes a noxious use or a nuisance? Is it always possible to identify the party with liability? What are the grounds on which one party in a land-use conflict is burdened with liability for damage to the interests of others that are given the protection of property?

In the gas station example, why is it that the owner of residential property has a right (created by zoning) to peace and quiet? Why should the owner of the gas station site not have a right to the enjoyment of the income that would accrue from the provision of valued services to customers at a convenient site? Does the peace and quiet of a residential neighborhood have some a priori superiority over the convenience to automobile owners?

Why should the owners of property on top of coal deposits be guaranteed freedom from subsidence? Why should they be allowed to limit the technology of coal mining to a less efficient method of recovery that will in turn raise the cost of coal to consumers and make them bear the burden of higher prices or less warmth in winter?

The regulation of air and water pollution, under the police power, is a public activity that is increasingly important. Why should downstream or downwind population be protected against pollution if this raises the costs of providing goods and services at lower costs to the population generally?

Justice Brandeis's arguments in the *Pennsylvania Coal* v. *Mahon* case really advance conflicting principles in connection with the equity and efficiency aspects of the case. He argues, on the one hand, that legislation must take into account, not the value of the coal alone but the value of the surface land as well. He then goes on to say, however, that while reciprocity of advantage is important where the restriction of a landowner's use of property is imposed to confer a public *benefit*, it is not a controlling consideration where the restriction is accomplished to "protect the public from detriment and danger." What is "detriment and danger"? Is the noise and activity of a gas station in a residential neighborhood a "detriment and danger"? What about the possibility of subsidence? What about air or water pollution?

The initial reaction is to say that all these effects of particular types of land use are detriments and/or dangers. But is the unavailability of a convenient gas station a detriment or danger to the motorist? Is the higher price of coal a detriment or danger to the coal consumers of the community? Air- and water-pollution-control equipment cost a great deal of money that is passed on to consumers in the form of higher prices. If we are really concerned about air pollution, why are there so few regulations about cigarette smoking in public places? How does the public decide which detriments and dangers will be given priority?

Noise control, the avoidance of subsistence, and the control of air and water pollution could all be looked upon as legitimate activities of government under the police power to protect the public from detriment and danger. They can also, however, be looked upon as restrictions placed on some persons to confer benefits on others.

There is always a reciprocity of advantage, as Justice Brandeis noted, to burdened individuals from living in a civilized community. The imposition of social judgments on acceptable and unacceptable types of benefits and detriments inevitably has distributional effects. It also tends to have the effect of removing the resolution of conflicts from individual negotiation and substituting comprehensive social control over human activities.

The policy implications of the preceding discussion are far-reaching. Zoning and other land-use regulations are no longer restricted in their application to municipalities for the segregation of noncompatible land uses. The advent of land-use plans on a statewide basis will result in the designation of all land for particular uses. Such plans will remove conflicts of interest from individual or local control. An objective of many land-use plans is the restriction of any development on some types of land and the intensification of development on other types of land. Should these decisions be removed from the individualistic decision-making of the market?

The building of an airport or a freeway deprives some owners of their land (with just compensation) and may create enormous increases in value for adjacent property owners. The classification of some land for open space may deprive its owners of practically all its value. The public gets the benefit of the open space, and there is no reciprocity of advantage for the landowners deprived of any development potential (other than the advantage of residing in a civilized community). Thus the changes in property values resulting directly from the allocational decisions of the state have powerful effects on income distribution in the community and at the same time remove decisions from the marketplace where efficiency would be served by negotiations that necessitated explicit valuations of differing land uses.

Zoning deals with problems growing out of the use of private property as a mechanism for control of land use. Whether it is the most efficient or equitable means of dealing with these problems is an open question that we will address again in subsequent chapters.

Notes

1. *Pennsylvania Coal* v. *Mahon*, 260 U.S. 393 (1922). *Village of Euclid* v. *Ambler Realty*, 272 U.S. 365 (1926).

2. One city that has used private covenants rather than zoning to control land use is Houston, Texas. For a generally favorable account of the results, see Bernard Siegan, "Non-Zoning in Houston," *Journal of Law and Economics* 71 (1970): 71-147.

6

The Economics
of Land

The price of land and the use of land are controlled by economic forces. Those forces of course are structured by the forms of property rights, zoning, taxation, and other laws affecting land use. But when all is said and done, a particular parcel of land, with its advantages and disadvantages, sells or rents for the price people are willing to pay for it. And it will be used in ways that reflect the price people are willing to pay for it.

One could grow corn on Manhattan Island, or locate high-rise office buildings in the middle of Iowa. Why doesn't it happen? Because land on Manhattan is too valuable as officespace. And because no one would pay the price for officespace in Iowa necessary to cover the costs of skyscrapers.

Demand for Land

The price of land depends on what people are willing to pay for it—on the demand. The supply of all land is, for practical purposes, fixed by the geographic confines of the United States. But the supply of any particular kind of land depends on the price people are willing to pay for it being high enough to justify its conversion from the existing use. Thus farmland will be converted to residential land if people are willing to pay more for its residential use than farm use by a sufficient margin to cover the costs of street, sewers, and so on.

The demand for land is determined by four basic factors: population, income, preferences, and technology. Population is obvious. People must have food to eat (which usually requires land to produce), living space, and a variety of other goods and services that take greater or lesser quantities of land to produce.

Income is an important determinant because of its effects on people's expenditure patterns. Higher incomes are usually accompanied by higher expenditures on food—not necessarily more, but better. It takes more land to raise a pound of meat than a loaf of bread. Rising incomes are particularly translated into demands for more house space and larger garden areas. Rising incomes are also translated into demands for vacation homes and recreation areas.

Preferences are related to incomes in the demand for land, but the relationships are not always direct. A Manhattan apartment-dweller occupies far less land than the hill farmer in Kentucky. And he may utilize Central Park far more intensively than the Kentuckian uses the Great Smokies. But it would appear that the demand for land is positively related to income—at least in the amount spent on land-based services.

Technology might be considered a factor determining the supply of land—rather than the demand. But for analytic purposes, it is useful to talk about how technology has affected the demand. Technology has been important in agriculture and silviculture in reducing the demand for land by increasing yields per acre through better seeds, fertilizer, insecticides, fungicides, and so on. Technology has also been instrumental in increasing the net output of agricultural land. Tractors do not necessitate the use of land for maintaining oxen. The farmer no longer needs a woodlot for fuel or fenceposts. Technology has released land formerly used for agriculture in the East or South to silviculture or even idle status.

Far and away the most significant technological change affecting the demand for land has been the automobile. The automobile has freed man from the necessity of living close enough to his work to walk or close enough to a mass-transit system to utilize it. The automobile has made suburban sprawl possible and revolutionized the way in which our culture lives, works, and plays.

Fifty years ago, the urban family that lived in a 1200-square-foot apartment in a four-story walk-up tenement might be directly responsible for 500 square feet of land area. Today's suburban family occupying a 1200-square-foot house on a 50- by 100-foot lot occupies ten times as much land directly. And indirectly, through parking requirements for the car at work, school, and shopping center and the streets and freeways necessary to new patterns of social and economic activity, the family may consume fifteen or twenty times as much land as a half-century earlier.

The demand for land depends on population, income, tastes, and technology, and most of those factors have joined to increase greatly the demand for land in the United States—particularly the demand for residential land and automobile-related space requirements for roads and parking.

The supply of land in the United States is fixed in the sense that the total number of acres is a constant. But the availability of any particular type of land can be increased by the conversion of other land. The conversion takes place when the expected income from the land in a more intensive use is greater than the income in a less intensive use plus the cost of improvements.

Economic Rent and Land Price

How do supply and demand operate to control the price of land? While this question can really be answered definitively only on a general-equilibrium basis, it is possible to distinguish the main influences. Let us begin our explanation with a single example for agricultural land. Suppose that a particular acre of Kansas wheat land produces an average of 100 bushels of wheat per year when farmed in the most efficient manner. Assume that the average price received by the Kansas farmer for his wheat is $5 per bushel. The farmer's annual average total revenue per acre is $500.

Suppose further that when the farmer applies labor, tractor services, seed, fertilizer, and so on, up to the point where the last dollar of expenditure on any of these inputs produces just an additional dollar's worth of wheat, that his total costs are $400. How much would he be willing to pay as annual rent for the use of the land? $100 [the difference between the total revenue for the wheat ($500) and the cost of all the other inputs ($400).]

What would happen if the price of wheat fell? Or the price of labor rose? Or the cost per acre of tractor services fell? Or if better seeds increased yield per acre? The annual rent that the farmer would be willing to pay for the use of agricultural land would have as a maximum the difference between the cost of production of crops on that land and the revenue produced by their sale.

Another example is the demand for residential land. Many families in an urban area would like to live on a quarter-acre lot in a 2000-square-foot house. Land costs a certain amount to develop (for streets, sewers, and so on) and houses cost a certain amount to build (for carpenters, plumbers, lumber, nails, and so on) and the capital invested in a house will have an annual interest cost. Interest, amortization, repairs, insurance, taxes, and so on determine the annual costs of maintaining a capital investment in land development and house construction.

Families are willing to pay differing proportions of their disposable income for housing. Their effective demand will be translated into demands for structures of particular size and quality. It will also be translated into demands for space in particular neighborhoods that are convenient to work, schools, parks, and other amenities and conveniences.

The difference between the cost of the house structure—on an annual basis—and the annual expenditure that a family is willing to make on it—will accrue to the owner of the land as a "rent."

In economic theory, the difference between the cost of producing goods or services and the price that people are willing to pay for those services is a rent. Rent accrues to the owners of certain types of land because that land is particularly well suited for the production of a good or service relative to the alternative land or methods of production available.

When we say that "rent accrues to the owners," we need to note the role of expectations (to be discussed). The owner of land converted from, say, agricultural to residential use, may sell it to a speculator at a price that reflects its value in agricultural production. The speculator in turn may sell it to a developer at a price that represents some of the capitalized value of the rents that the ultimate users (the homeowners) will pay for its residential use. The ultimate owner pays the capitalized value of the rents in the purchase price of the house, and they appear to him as part of the cost of home ownership.

Rents represent the difference between the market price of services or goods produced with the assistance of land (house space or crops) and the costs of the variable inputs of labor and capital.

Consider our earlier agricultural example. The land in question produced a surplus of wheat revenue over the cost of wheat production of $100 per year. Suppose that on an adjoining parcel of land of less fertility that the application of labor, tractor services, fertilizer, and so on produced an output of only 80 bushels per acre so that costs of $400 per year were matched by revenues of only $400 per year (80 bushels times $5 per bushel). The land would yield no surplus of revenue over cost in wheat production — it would yield no rent. (It would, in fact, be farmed less intensively to maximize rent.)

The rent in question is a measure of the resources saved for society by the use of the superior land. It is possible to raise 20 bushels more wheat per acre on the superior land than on the inferior land with the same application of labor, tractor services, fertilizer, seed, and so on. The rent that accrues to the land is a measure of the social saving of scarce resources gained by using it rather than inferior land.

Consider the housing example. Suppose that a family is willing to spend $2000 dollars per year of disposable income for a home and that construction costs (indicating an annual capital cost of $1000 per annum) for the same house are identical on two parcels of land, but one parcel is 20 miles closer to the urban center where the homeowner must commute each working day.

The prospective homeowner estimates that the extra commutation costs for 40 miles per day for 250 days per year are 10¢ per mile or an annual cost differential of $1000 (250 times 40 times 10¢). Other things being equal, the family would be willing to spend $1000 per year more to occupy the house closer to the urban center in order to avoid the commutation costs. The rent accruing to the site closer to the urban center on which the house was located would receive a differential rent of $1000 per year more than the remoter house site.

Rent accrues to the owners of land that has superior location or productivity for the production of goods and services. The rent is a measure of the savings available from using one site rather than another. This is a key concept for the efficient allocation of resources. The maximization of rents leads to the greatest social output of goods and services available from existing resources and technology.

Rents depend on the demand for the services or goods produced and the variable costs (labor, tractor services, nails) of producing the services in question. An increase in the demand for wheat that raised its price would increase the rent on wheat land. A rise in the price of labor, tractor services, or seed would increase the cost of wheat production and reduce the rent.

An increase in disposable incomes or a change in tax laws that increased the amount that people spend on housing would be expected to increase rents on housing sites. A decline in transportation costs would be expected to increase rents on remoter sites and decrease rents on sites that were closer in.

Capitalization of Rent

Thus far our discussion of rents has been in terms of annual costs. The price of land, when it is purchased rather than rented, represents the capitalization of *expected* rents into a capital sum. When people purchase land, they *expect* that there will be a series of rents accruing to the land in the future. The purchase price is a payment for the right to receive these rents.

The right to receive future "rent" payments is one of the rights in the bundle of rights that is exchanged when property in land is sold by one party to another. The farmer who purchases superior agricultural land may think of the purchase as the purchase of rights to receive the difference between his production costs and revenue from the sale of crops in the future. The homeowner may think of the house purchase as the purchase of the right to live in the residence in the future and avoid the payment of monthly house rent to someone else. But both are purchasing the right to an expected income or imputed income or the avoidance of a cost in the future.

How much will people be willing to pay for the rights to expected future income from land? This depends on their expectations and the rate at which they discount them for future receipt. A convenient formula to summarize these relationships is given below:

$$P = \sum_{i=1}^{n} \frac{R_n - C_n}{(1 + i)^n}$$

where

P = price a purchaser would be willing to pay for a parcel of land

R = total revenues from the land-based economic activity in year n

C = costs of producing the land-based services in year n

i = interest cost

n = year in which incomes and costs are received and incurred

Thus suppose that the farmer from our earlier example expects that his costs and prices for wheat next year and every succeeding year will be the same as this year so that the difference will always be $100 per acre. Assume that he can either lend or borrow money at a 10-percent interest rate. Substituting the numbers into the formula,

$$P = \Sigma \; \frac{(\$500 - \$400)}{(1 + 0.10)^1} \; + \; \frac{(\$500 - \$400)}{(1 + 0.10)^2} \; + \; \frac{(\$500 - \$400)}{(1 + 0.10)^3}$$

$$+ \; \ldots \; + \; \frac{(\$500 - \$400)}{(1 + 0.10)^n}$$

or

$$P = \Sigma \; \$90.91 \; + \; \$82.64 \; + \; \$68.49 \; + \; \ldots \; + \; 0 \; (\text{as } n = \infty)$$

(The value of P approaches $1000 as n approaches ∞.) The sum of this infinite series approaches $1000—the price the farmer or a landlord who bought the land for an investment would be willing to pay to acquire the right to receive a rent in perpetuity. If the rights to receive the rent from the land in perpetuity were accompanied with the expectation that the net return $R - C$ would be constant, the formula would be

$$P = \frac{R - C}{i}$$

Consider the logic of the formula in another way. If a person puts $1000 in a savings account, he would draw $100 interest per year on his capital at 10 percent. If he put $1000 into the purchase of the acre of land, he would receive an expected rent of $100 for its use next year. He would be willing to pay $1000 for land because it produced $100 per year, which is the return he could receive from an alternative investment.[1]

It is the objective of maximizing the present value of rents that controls the decisions about land use. The owner has the economic incentive to use his land in the way that will produce the highest rents. This involves using it to produce the goods and services most highly valued by the public (and reflected in prices) by the lowest cost (most efficient) methods. For this reason we would not expect the Manhattan landowner to grow corn or the Iowa landowner to supply skyscraper officespace to the public.

There is a very important point to be made here relative to the intertemporal allocation of land and other natural resources—to their conservation or exploitation. The land or natural-resource owner has a property right to the stream of income that may accrue from the economic use of the asset over time. Therefore he has a self-interest in maximizing his income from the land, not only in the present but in the future. If he manages the asset to increase his income in the present at the expense of the future, he has to take into account the realized value of present income versus the foregone value of future income. As noted in chapter 3, the exploitation of open access resources arises from the inability of an individual owner to compare present and future income because he has no certain claim to future income.

One of the alleged problems in current land-use discussions is the conversion of farmland to more intensive use. When the argument against conversion is a future shortage of food and agricultural land, the implicit economic argument is that present owners are either unaware that food prices will sharply increase agricultural rents in the future or that the interest rate used by farmland owners to discount future rents is lower than the social time rate of discount.

Private property and the operation of markets do create incentives for owners to use land and natural resources to produce goods and services most highly valued by society in the present. They also furnish an incentive for the conservation of resources until the time at which their use is most valuable for society.[2]

We have now outlined the basic theory to explain the price of land through the capitalization of expected rents. The theory needs a great deal of elaboration to approach the complexities of land market behavior. In conclusion there are four elements that have been instrumental in shaping the behavior of land prices in the United States in the recent past: expectations, taxation, financing, and marginal cost.

Expectations and Land Prices

Sometimes land prices are explained in terms of *expected* changes in the general price level. People have increasingly come to expect inflation, and land is often touted as a good hedge against inflation. Actually, land is no better as a hedge against inflation than any other real (as opposed to monetary) asset during a time of general inflation. If land prices were to increase at the same rate as a composite index of all prices, the real value of land assets (market price adjusted by inflation index) would not increase or decrease during a time of general inflation. Land or other any other real asset is only a better store of value during inflation than assets denominated in money terms such as currency, bank accounts, bonds, or life-insurance policies.

It is the expectation that land will increase in price faster than other real assets over time that has resulted in the rapid increase in land prices during recent years. In a long-run equilibrium situation, land prices cannot increase more rapidly than the net rents that accrue to land from its increasing scarcity. It is *expectations* about the increasing scarcity of urban, suburban, agricultural, industrial, seashore, or forest land relative to the demands for it that has led to increases in its market price relative to other real assets because of expectations about rising net rents.

An understanding of the recent behavior of land prices really depends on an understanding of the operation of assets markets. Sophisticated investors regard land as just one of a number of alternative investment opportunities. They sell other assets and purchase land when the expected returns from net rents on land, plus appreciation, exceed the income plus appreciation they expect to realize from stocks, bonds, commodities, or other investments.

It is the movement into and out of assets that leads to fluctuations in their prices and equalization in their returns. Thus suppose that because of shortage or inflation, the net rents accruing to apartment owners started to increase while the coupon interest payments accruing to holders of government bonds were fixed contractually. It would be expected that some investors would start selling bonds to take advantage of the higher return on their capital available from its investment in apartments. As they sold their bonds, the price of the bonds would fall—reflecting the increase in the supply of bonds for sale and the decrease in the demand for bonds by present and potential bondholders. On the other hand, increased demand would push apartment prices up.

The fall in the market value of bonds and the rise in the market price of apartments would continue until the coupon payments to bondholders, as a percentage return on the market price of the bonds, were equal to the net rental payments accruing to the apartment owners as a percentage return on the market price of apartments.

Actually, the role of expectations is more complicated than the scenario just outlined. If some investors *anticipate* that rising rents for apartments will drive up their market prices, they anticipate the gains that may occur in those prices and count the increase in the prices of the apartments as part of the return on their investment. Conversely, they may anticipate the fall in the market price of bonds as decreasing the effective return on their investment in bonds. Anticipations may hasten the adjustment of relative prices of the two capital assets—bonds and apartments.

An example may make this clear. Suppose that in an initial equilibrium situation an investor is receiving $1000 per year net return from an apartment that he owns and for which he paid the current market price of $10,000. Suppose he is also receiving $1000 per year as the coupon interest from a bond for which he paid the current market price of $10,000. He is receiving a return of 10 percent on both the apartment and the bond.

Then suppose that an increase in the demand for apartments by renters drives the returns from apartment ownership up to $1100 per year—representing a return on the original investment of 11 percent. The prices of apartments generally rise by 10 percent reflecting the rise in returns. The market price of our investor's apartment rises from $10,000 to $11,000. In the year in which the increase occurs, our investor realizes not only $1100 in rental return but an increase in the capital value of the apartment of $1000 for a total return of $2100 or 21 percent on his original $10,000 investment. The apartment has been a much better investment this year than bonds on which he is earning only 10 percent.

Having experienced such a favorable return on apartments (relative to bonds), suppose that our investor anticipates that the net rental returns on the apartment the following year will rise again and, along with them, the market price of the apartment will rise also. He (and other prescient investors) sells his bond and tries to buy more apartments. This drives down the price of bonds and drives up the price of apartments and leads to further anticipations of capital gains from apartments and capital losses from bonds. The process goes on until the market prices of bonds have gone so low and the market prices of apartments have gone so high that the coupon rate on bonds represents a very attractive return on the market price of bonds and the net rental income from apartments represents an unattractive return on the market price of apartments.

At some point, investors start to anticipate the return of the pendulum and try to get out of apartments and into bonds and their sales of apartments and purchases of bonds reverse the upward trend in market prices for apartments and the downward trend in the market prices for bonds. As soon as bonds are appreciating and apartments are depreciating in market prices, the changes in prices are taken into account in rates of return on investment.

Anticipations quicken the pace of market adjustments and may cause them to overshoot equilibrium. Real estate prices are determined by expectations of future changes in economic rents. And because there has been so much talk about the impending scarcity of land and natural resources, real estate markets may have overanticipated the rise.

Taxation and Land Prices

The incidence and structure of taxes and subsidies has a very substantial effect on the behavior of land markets relative to other asset markets. Since any tax or subsidy increases or decreases the net rent accruing to the owner of real estate, it affects the prices of real estate that reflect the capitalization of these rents.

There is one tax that may decrease the value of real estate relative to other assets — property tax. Property taxes are levied by municipalities, water, school, flood control, fire-protection districts, and by a large variety of geographically defined and property-tax-based public authorities.

It can be argued that the services provided by these districts increase the value of property located in them. There is evidence that land in areas with good public services is worth more because of the availability of schools, libraries, parks, garbage collection, fire protection, and so on. It is also true that these services could be provided by alternative revenue sources.

A property tax is levied on the assessed value of property. Assessments are based on a variety of formulas that usually have some relation to the market price of the land which in turn bears some relationship to the income accruing to the owner of the land. To the extent that property taxes represent a cost of land ownership, they decrease the net rents that accrue to landowners, and hence they decrease the market price of land that represents the capitalization of those rents.

Since investments in stocks or bonds or machinery are not taxed on the basis of capital value but actual income, property tax may lessen the returns on land relative to investments in stocks, bonds, savings accounts, and other investments.

Most other current tax laws tend to increase the value of land relative to other assets. Income taxes are not levied on the imputed value of housing services received by homeowners from tenancy of their own residences. Since the value of housing services consumed by the average American homeowner is on the order of 20-40 percent of income, this is a considerable item.

Real estate taxes and the interest on home mortgages are deductible from gross personal income in the calculation of federal income tax. The practical effect of this is to decrease the federal tax liability in direct proportion to the size of the property owner's marginal tax rate, mortgage interest, and property-tax liability.

It is true that the interest paid to finance the purchase or holding of other forms of assets (stocks, bonds, commodities, objets d'art) is equally deductible from taxable income in the calculation of tax liabilities. What is different with land is that the income from the personal consumption of land services is not subject to taxation. The income-redistributional effect of this is to subsidize (by the reduction of income-tax liability) the use of land by high-income taxpayers in direct proportion to the income and the share of their wealth held in the form of land. Its effect on the allocation of income between various uses is to increase the demand for land by higher income individuals.

While a number of assumptions and qualifications to the analysis are necessary, it can be stated that the present operation of tax laws substantially reduces the after-tax costs of home ownership and thereby increases the net value of the imputed rent that a homeowner capitalizes into the value of a home.

Financing Land

One of the most important determinants of the operation of land markets, relative to other asset markets, is the scope allowed small investors for

financing purchase (speculation) on small equity margins. A small investor
will have great difficulty in borrowing money at low interest rates for the
purchase of stocks and bonds in which he has little equity. On the other
hand, a prospective house or farm purchaser will be able to borrow from
75-100 percent of the purchase price of a residence or farm on a long-term
(up to 40-year mortgage) at an interest rate subsidized and held to artifi-
cially low levels by the government and with principal and interest
guaranteed to the lender.

Speculation in undeveloped land is often financed by contract sales in
which the contract is carried by the seller. Farmer Jones sells 100 acres to
developer Smith for $1000 per acre on a contract with 10 percent down and
the balance over 10 years at 8 percent interest. If the land appreciates more
than 8 percent per year, developer Smith will make a handsome return on
his initial small investment. (The government will even allow him to deduct
interest payments from his income for tax purposes.) If the land fails to ap-
preciate, he can always default on the contract or sell it to some other party.

The ease of financing land speculation by mortgage or contract borrowing has made it a popular investment for small investors with speculative intent. The government's tax policy has also made speculation attractive
because of the lower rate at which capital gains are taxed than income. The
dividends from stock or the interest from bonds when taken as income are
taxed at a high marginal rate while the capital gains from appreciation are
taxed at a lower rate.

The investment in a residence, apart from the advantages cited in the
preceding section, is attractive as a speculative investment because any
capital gains from its purchase and resale are exempt from even capital-
gains taxation if they are reinvested within eighteen months of sale in
another principal residence or realized after age 55. In what other investment can one take income in a nontaxable form (imputed income from
owner occupancy) and be subject to no capital-gains tax?

Marginal Costs and Land Values

The high price of agricultural land, relative to any net return from its use in
agriculture has frequently been a source of puzzlement. Why are farmers so
willing to pay high prices for adjoining land when it would appear from their
financial records that their net return per acre is so small on adjacent land?

There are probably two reasons for this phenomenon other than optimism about prices and yields and possible concealment of income and enjoyment of imputed income. The first reason is that many farmers think of
their own labor services as having a low market price because of lack of
alternative employment opportunities adjacent to their farm. They feel
"rooted" to their farm, and if they do have extra time, they are often not

able to sell their labor services to employers because the employers want full-time employees. Thus the farmer contemplating the purchase of a neighbor's land may consider the opportunity cost of his labor services (and/or his sons' and wife's) relatively low, which consequently tends to increase his estimation of the net economic rent he could produce from farming adjoining acres.

Second, agricultural technology in the last century and a half has developed bigger and costlier tractors, plows, combines, and all other manner of agricultural machinery with output capacities geared to *larger* units than many of the existing farms. Thus the marginal machine cost of tilling additional agricultural acres is seen as much lower than average cost by many farmers, which makes the net rent on adjoining acreage seem larger than the rents realized on existing holdings with existing technology.

The process of land consolidation has tended to push up the price of land because the marginal costs of labor and machinery for neighboring farmers have been estimated to be lower than the average costs for existing land. Established farmers are able to make a profit on the historical cost of their land, but new farmers would find that the market price of land precluded their realization of a normal rate of return on investment capital.

If all farmers were to sell their land, the average price that investors with mobile capital and labor would pay would be lower than the marginal price now determined by neighboring farmers who have capital and labor services available at what they believe are low marginal costs. Farmlands untilled by their owners are usually leased on fairly favorable terms by their neighbors, and when lands are sold, they are often sold to neighboring farmers.

This analysis is not meant to explain all the high price of farmland relative to its reported average net economic rent. There is undoubtedly a preference for farmland as an investment that has deep psychological and sociological roots. There is also the history and expectation of the conversion of farmland to more intensive uses that breeds optimism about returns for investment. Nevertheless, the prices of farmland behave in ways that are difficult to explain solely from farm records on the costs and returns from agricultural use.

Summary

This chapter has attempted a simple exposition and summary of some of the major determinants of the operation of the markets for land. It has utilized a marginal-productivity theory of the employment of factors of production to explain the existence and nature of rents. It has made land prices a function of expectations about the net economic rents accruing to the owners of particular parcels of land. It has not evaluated the determinants of the demand for land or the effects on controlling the use of land. The public policy determinants of the supply of land and the demand for it are considered in the next chapter.

Notes

1. Readers wishing a more extensive account of rents and their capitalization into land values will find a detailed account in Paul A. Samuelson, *Economics,* 11th ed. (New York: McGraw-Hill, 1980), chap. 28, 30.

2. Robert Solow has demonstrated elegantly that secure property rights, knowledge of the future, and efficient markets would result in the rationing of resource use to produce the greatest social value available over time from exhaustible natural resources. See R.M. Solow, "The Economics of Resources or the Resources of Economics," *American Economic Review* 64 (no. 2) (May 1974). However, Solow's demonstration does not resolve the necessity for making social-value judgments about the rate of resource use over time that are bound up in the rate of interest as a measure of time preference. The social character of "conservation" as a judgment on the time rate of use of resources is thoughtfully analyzed in S. Ciriacy-Wantrup, *Resource Conservation Economics and Policies* (Berkeley, Calif.): University of California, Division of Agricultural Sciences, 1963).

7

Public Policies and Private Uses of Land

The preceding chapter considered the way in which the market for land operates to determine prices and uses. Advocates of land-use planning find the outcomes of the market objectionable in a variety of ways. The objective of land-use planning is to modify the present operations of the market. How will this be done? What will be the effects—intentional and unintentional?

The demands for land-based services determine the derived demands for land. There are four main determinants of the demand for land-based services: population, income, tastes, and technology. Land-use planning can do little to affect the first two. Its effects on tastes and technology operate via their effects on relative prices over longer periods of time.

Affluence may be directed toward larger houses and lots, more manufactured products, and commercial facilities. It most certainly has been reflected, at least in the United States, in demands for parks, golf courses, tennis courts, recreational homes, and open spaces for recreational purposes. That is not true to the same extent in some affluent, land-scarce, European countries.

Over the longer run, tastes and technology are very important determinants of the demand for land. Eating meat rather than cereal is a cultural decision. So is living in a suburban home rather than a high-rise apartment or playing golf rather than bridge.

On the other hand, agricultural technology has made it possible to use some lands that were unusable and to use others better. High-rise apartments depend on engineering. From the golf cart to the outboard motor, technology has affected even the recreational use of land.

Land-use planning per se can do only one thing to limit the demand for land. It can limit the amount of land necessitated for streets, highways, utility rights-of-way, and shopping centers by limiting urban sprawl. Land-use planning operates basically by limiting and reallocating the uses of land. Land-use planning supplements the use of price as an allocative mechanism. One might say that the prohibition of the use of a particular piece of land is the equivalent of putting an infinite price on it for that use.

Land-use planning and control operates primarily on the supply side. The essence of land-use planning is reallocating the supply of land between uses, administratively, rather than relying on the operation of the market. The reallocation of land uses will increase the supply of land available for some uses and decrease the supply available for other uses and thereby change the prices of both. In the absence of any sort of land-use controls, land prices would have much less dispersion around a mean because of the potential substitutability of higher intensity uses for lower intensity uses.

One might regard the designation of land uses as a way of increasing the prices of higher intensity use land by limiting its supply and decreasing the prices of lower intensity use land by increasing its supply and permanently dampening increases in its price through speculation.

That this is generally realized can be inferred from a consideration of the usual stances of interest groups on controversies over changes in zoning and use plans at the local, state, or national levels.[1] Farmers might be expected to favor land-use planning since it will tend to lower the costs of agricultural land with development potential. But the farmers are also landowners and so they generally oppose any legislative changes that limit their ability to realize capital gains from land sales.

At the local level, businessmen's groups usually press for increases in the supply of land zoned for residential, commercial, or industrial development since reductions in the relative price of land are thought to stimulate local growth and business.

Environmentalists favor restrictions on the development of (other people's) land since it provides them with a valuable amenity at no direct cost to themselves and, depending on their residential location, may raise the value of their land.

One of the ironies of the arguments cited for land-use planning is the contribution that government policies and regulations have made to so many of the extant problems. Urban sprawl is a good example. Consider the government policies that have increased the demand for residential land. Taxation and finance arrangements have already been considered in the preceding chapter.

Zoning

Zoning regulations are a prime contributor to the increase in the demand for land. When zoning laws set minimum lot sizes, they increase the amount of land necessary for housing. The effect of the large lot sizes required by many suburban communities is to segregate lower income groups from the community by raising the cost of the land necessary for a single house or housing unit. There is an economic as well as social rationale for these policies. Holding down the size of the population and increasing the income level of the population in a suburban town can reduce expenditures on schools, police, and social services relative to the taxable value. Taxable value might increase through smaller lot zoning that would permit more houses but the increase in population-determined demand for social services might rise faster.

Minimum lot sizes are an important contributor to low-density suburban sprawl. So are provisions for set-backs, side yards, maximum house-space/lot-size requirements, and wide-street and off-street parking provisions. All these regulations of course are promulgated to provide environmental amenities. Their effect is to increase the demand for land.

Consider a typical suburban zoning ordinance: Suppose that houses are subject to 20-foot setback provisions, front and rear, and 20-foot side yards. A 1200-square foot, single-story house will require a minimum 5600-square-foot, lot. Suppose, on the other hand, that the same house were built as a row house with no side yards and a 10-foot setback in front of the house. The homes could have identical size back gardens, and the townhouse would occupy less than 50 percent of the area of the other. The potential land saving in streets must also be considered since they presently also take 25 percent to 30 percent of the land area of a residential development.[2]

In recent years many exurban areas have begun to mandate 1-, 2-, 5-, 10-, or 20-acre minimums for housing development. This systematically increases the demand for rural acreage that will be used for residential rather than agricultural uses.

There are two final ironies to large-lot zoning. The per-acre price of the land, determined by its net rents, is reduced. As we saw in the preceding chapter, the diminution in the value of net rents is a measure of the loss of "social saving." And the area of land that must be used and the costs of streets, highways, sewers, and other public utilities is increased.

One of the arguments for land-use planning, often cited by its proponents, is the existence of "leap-frog developments"—idle land amid developed land.[3] This phenomenon is blamed on speculation. One of the contributing factors to this phenomenon, however, is premature zoning for higher intensity use before there is an effective demand for it. If, for example, land is zoned industrial or commercial, there may be a surplus of this type of land available. Yet the price of the land may preclude its use for residential or agricultural use. Residential developments frequently leap-frog agricultural areas in search of cheaper land. The agricultural land is bid up in price, and farming is no longer an economic use of it. Yet it may also not be "ripe" for development.

The use of zoning and its attendant effects on market prices can affect the timing of utilization. As discussed in the previous chapter, an owner is economically rational to delay the development of land if it is increasing more rapidly in value than the costs of carrying it.

The example cited in the previous chapter makes this clear. If a farmer can sell an acre for $1000, he can put it in the bank and earn a certain interest, say 8 percent, on the purchase price. On the other hand, if the land is increasing more rapidly than 8 percent, plus or minus net rents or carrying costs, he will be economically rational to postpone development until the net return, including appreciation, falls below what he could realize by development.

Uncertainty is the great enemy of rational land-use decisions. Uncertainty operates to decrease the time-discounted value of expected future returns for a parcel of undeveloped or underdeveloped land. The owner may therefore decide to develop it for a lower intensity use than might be justified and preclude future land-use decisions.

There is evidence that this has happened in California as a result of uncertainties about future development that would be permitted by the California coastal commissions.

Certainty, on the other hand, is the great contributor to economically rational land-use decisions. If the best use for land will be open space or agricultural land at some time in the future, its designation for that use will prohibit irreversible development. If, on the other hand, the best future use of a parcel might be intensive residential or industrial, its designation will make its price too high for low-density residential use and preclude its development along those lines.

Taxation

One means by which development of land can be accelerated or delayed is taxation. Taxation increases the costs of owning land and thereby decreases the net rents accruing to the owner. Thus if farmland is taxed at a lower rate than residential land, the net rents accruing to its owner in farm use are larger than they otherwise would be and conversion to residential use is delayed until the rents from residential use have risen sufficiently to compensate for the tax.

Farmland is taxed at a preferential rate in many areas of the United States. The original rationale for doing this was that farmland required fewer police, fire-protection, and school services than residences on a land value basis. Taxes were implicitly adjusted to conform more closely to the per capita or per-capita income receipt of services than they would have been if levied solely on the basis of land value. There was, in fact, a recognition that a tax based on real estate values was a good proxy for income in a wholly agricultural community but not in a mixed community because of the higher ratio of capital to income in agriculture.

Attempts to delay the conversion of agricultural land by deferral of tax and taxation at a lower rate as long as the land remains in agricultural use have been tried in a number of states.[4] The general conclusion to be drawn is that the delay has been minimal and that the tax deferment merely aided speculative holders by reducing their holding costs and allowing their payment at the time of conversion from agricultural to residential use. Another inference to be drawn, however, is that the value placed by the public on land for residential use is very much higher than the present or future value placed on that land for agricultural purposes.

Utility Pricing and Sprawl

It is frequently alleged that the price of land converted from agricultural to residential use is higher than its real social value because of the subsidization of construction of new schools, highway and public utility systems by existing urban taxpayers. The argument is made that these services are provided on an average cost basis by all taxpayers rather than a marginal cost basis to the users of the new facilities necessitated by urban sprawl. To the extent that this is true in the pricing of these public services, newly converted land is overvalued because of the lessened incidence of taxes and user charges for public utilities on the net rents accruing to the owners of the land. Any form of restriction placed on the use of land or any change in the patterns of taxation, subsidy, or public service user charges will be reflected in changes in the patterns of economic rents and hence in land prices.

The redistribution of the costs of public services and the consequent change in rents and land values is an element in one of the frequently cited arguments for land-use planning: the containment of urban sprawl. The advantages cited for curtailment of urban growth are the reduction in the costs of providing public services and the provision of environmental amenities for the residents of an urban area by the retention of a rural "greenbelt" close to intensive residential development. It should be noted that these are real savings of capital and labor services that would allow their use elsewhere in the economy for the provision of productive services.

The designation of a "greenbelt," however, would result in substantial redistribution of property values. In an equilibrium setting, the net rents within the urban area thus contained should increase because of the lowered per-capita cost of providing public services and the increase in environmental amenities available to the population from the surrounding greenbelt. Property values, both developed and undeveloped, within the urban area should increase.

Property values in the greenbelt should fall, reflecting the loss of speculative value premised on future, more intensive development. The land available for development would be reduced in area and would rise sharply in value and, as a consequence, the land element in the price of housing services would rise. Part of this increase would represent the decrease in the cost of public services that would increase rents. Part of it would reflect increased scarcity. And part of it would reflect the increase in environmental amenity.

The diminution in value of the greenbelt land would also have three contributing elements—all from the reduction in speculative value. First, there would be the loss of scarcity rents that had been shifted to the land still available for development. Second, there would be the loss of the rents that had reflected the potential shifting of incremental costs of public services to the urban area. And, third, some of the environmental amenity provided by the greenbelt and paid for by suburban purchasers in their net rents, is shifted to the owners of the urban land from the owners of the greenbelt land.

A successfully designed land-use plan to concentrate urban development by containing development inside "greenbelt" areas could increase the total welfare of a community by the reduction in the costs of public services and the increase of environmental amenities for the residents. The redistribution of wealth from the owners of greenbelt land to the owners of urban land creates powerful pressures to block this measure in the absence of compensation for losses to the affected owners.[5]

Any society engages in some form of land-use control and planning. The control and planning mechanisms run along a continuum from private negotiations and transactions to central authoritarian specification of each and every use of land. In between are such measures as zoning, which designates uses and standards and relies on negative prohibitions (rather than positive specifications) on any change in land use.

To illustrate the continuum, Los Angeles County could sanction and enforce any voluntary contractual agreements among its landowners for the use of land. Or it could "zone" the county with certain sections having permitted uses, density limitations, setback and height limitations, and so on. Or it could prohibit any change or development without official permit on a case-by-case basis. Or it could, positively, order landowners to use land in specific ways under threat of criminal sanction.

What types of control on land-use decisions *should* be used? What kinds of tax and pricing policies for the provision of public services *should* be used to affect land use in socially desirable ways? Answers to those questions depend on some identification of priorities for the use and enjoyment of land.

Notes

1. An astute analysis of the state-level politics of land-use planning may be found in R. Kenneth Godwin and W. Bruce Shepard, "State Land Use Policy: Winners and Losers," unpublished mimeo (Corvallis, Oregon: Oregon State University, 1974).

2. For estimates of costs of alternative residential patterns, see Real Estate Research Corporation, *The Cost of Sprawl: Environmental and Economic Costs of Alternative Residential Development Patterns at the Urban Fringe* (Washington, D.C.: Government Printing Office, 1974).

3. Mason Gaffney, "Tax Reform to Release Land" in *Modernizing Urban Land Policy,* ed. Marion Clawson, (Baltimore: John Hopkins University Press for Resources for the Future, 1973).

4. For a survey, see U.S. Department of Agriculture, Economic Research Service, *State Programs for the Differential Assessment of Farm and Open Space Land* (Washington, D.C.: Government Printing Office, 1974).

5. These problems were considered explicitly in the English Town and County Planning Act (1947). For a variety of reasons, the attempt to recoup the gains in land values resulting from planning and compensate the losers has been unsuccessful. See Daniel R. Mandelker, "Notes from the English: Compensation in Town and Country Planning," *California Law Review* 49 (1961). For a more acerbic view of the problem of redistributing wealth and welfare in urban planning, see Mason Gaffney, "Welfare Economics and the Environment," in *Environmental Quality in a Growing Economy,* ed. Henry Jarrett, (Baltimore: Johns Hopkins University Press, 1966).

The Evaluation of Alternative Land-Use-Control Systems

The institutions that control land use control human behavior. They determine wealth and income. They affect life, liberty, and property. The increase of population, the development of land-consumptive technology, and an increased recognition of the importance of the environment have all contributed to a growing uncertainty about the contemporary adequacy of the institutions that determine land use in the United States.

Do we need new institutions to guide our choices about land use? Perhaps not "new" institutions as much as a refurbishment of old ones. It should not be surprising that the institutional framework for resource management developed to maximize physical output in an age of resource abundance and capital scarcity should need adjustment in a later period of relative capital abundance and natural resource scarcity.

Any set of institutions to allocate resource use has certain effects — to favor one group at the expense of another, to facilitate the exploitation of the environment rather than its preservation, to produce incomes for some and less expensive products for others.

The next chapter will spell out a set of concrete proposals for the control of land use. This chapter will develop a set of criteria for the evaluation of any set of land-use controls. These criteria will form the basis for the evaluations of the defects in existing land-use institutional arrangements and the merits of those proposed. The criteria may be treated under the headings of efficiency and equity.

Efficiency

Efficiency needs to be regarded in terms of principles and systems. A system or set of principles for land-use control could be said to be efficient if it would not be possible to reorganize the use of land in some way to increase the satisfaction of everyone. This is a Pareto-optimal criterion. Transactions to bring about Pareto-optimal improvements increase the welfare of all members of society.

Allocative efficiency is a traditional argument for the use of voluntary exchanges of property rights in a market context rather than the administrative assignment of use rights. The allocative efficiency of the market is held to arise from the ability of individuals to exchange use rights until they reach a distribution of use rights that represents a Pareto-optimal equilibrium.

By definition, a Pareto-optimal equilibrium occurs when no further exchange transactions could be made that would leave at least one party better off and no one else worse off. (In other words, one party would be in a "preferred" position and no other party in a "less preferred" condition).

There are several facets to the efficiency criterion. It is important that a land-use control system allocate land efficiently between uses, between persons, and between periods of time. It would be inefficient for some members of a society to devote land to growing wheat on a particular parcel of land if other members of that society were willing to pay much more for office space on the same parcel. It would be inefficient for a society to prevent the transfer from Smith to Jones of rights to use the office space if Jones were willing to pay more for the use of the resource. It would be inefficient for society to convert agricultural land to an office building now if that precluded the later construction of a high-rise office building that yielded much higher rents than one presently feasible or if agricultural land will later increase in value.

One fundamental assumption underlying the use of the market for the exchange of use rights in land is that all the uses or social benefits from a particular parcel of land can be isolated and controlled. Thus the inability of the owner of the wheatfield to sell the rights to visual amenity that it provides to adjoining property owners because of the high transactions costs that would be involved is an impediment to efficient allocation between uses. The rent produced by the land in wheat production is less than the rent produced from use as office space only because the owner cannot charge for the provision of environmental amenity. The conversion of the land from agriculture to office space appears to be efficient, that is, Pareto-optimal, only because the preferences for environmental amenity of the adjoining property owners have not been incorporated into the transaction over use rights because of high transactions costs.

A second fundamental assumption underlying the use of the market for the exchange of use rights is that money is an appropriate standard for the interpersonal comparison of benefits. If office renters are willing to pay more than wheat consumers for the use of land, that choice is assumed to represent a valid judgment on the relative merit of competing claims for resource use, even if the wheat consumers are starving and the office-space consumers are idle rich. Because the assignment of property rights determines income distribution as well as efficient use allocation of resources, the market has always been subject to social modification.

The third assumption underlying the use of the market for allocating the time pattern of resource allocation is that the interest rate that individuals use to discount future use is an appropriate social judgment on present versus future use. The time preference of the individual is increased by risk and uncertainty that are not a consideration for society as a whole. Thus the market may discount the future use of resources at a higher rate than society and this may result in premature exhaustion or conversion of natural resources.[1]

The belief that the market will operate to produce Pareto-optimal allocation between uses and persons over time is based on a number of restrictive assumptions. The lack of realism of the assumptions, or their unacceptability as a basis for allocation has led to extensive restructuring of the institutions for resource use.

Our political and economic system is substantially based on individual choice. We believe that individuals should be entitled to allocate their incomes between alternative uses to satisfy their wants and needs in ways that they judge to be most satisfactory. Our present system of land-use control offers some scope for the exercise of individual choices. It is deficient in its provision for those who might wish to exchange income for environmental quality.

A second defect of our present land-use control system is cost distortion. The exercise of individual choices should be made within a framework that reflects real costs. A system that allows Smith to choose to use land at a low cost and thereby precludes Jones from using it in a way that produces goods and services highly valued by the rest of society is wasteful. It implicitly allows Smith to use resources at low cost that other members of society value more highly. A framework for choice needs to reflect the social costs of alternatives to the individual who chooses them.

Let us illustrate this point with reference to the example used in chapter 5 of the gas station in the residential neighborhood. A land-use control system (such as zoning) that precludes a gas station causes motorists to incur extra costs (in time, mileage) to secure gas and repairs for their cars. It increases the satisfaction that homeowners derive from peace and quiet. Is the value of the peace and quiet to the homeowners, equivalent to the costs to the motorists? If it is not, a zoning system precludes an exchange that could leave both parties better off.

Let us consider a different example. Suppose that certain land is zoned for agricultural use only, precluding the residential development that would otherwise take place. The best agricultural use is wheat that yields a rent of $100 per acre per year. The economic rent resulting from residential use would be $1000 per year. The rent in both cases represents the value of the goods (wheat or housing sites) over their cost of production (costs of labor and capital) (see chapter 6). A system of land-use controls that prevents residential use is preventing the exercise of choice that would leave society as a whole $900 per acre per year richer.

There may be good reasons for the decisions that are not reflected in the examples. An expected future scarcity of food may change the future rents from agricultural use. Or present agricultural use may provide benefits to the surrounding residents in the form of views and solitude for which they would be willing to pay but do not.

The rent accruing to the land in residential use may be overstated because the sewer system serving the subdivision may not be charged to the new residents at its incremental costs. Or the increased air pollution resulting from their commutation to the city center may not be included in the overall assessment of the costs of the new subdivision.

The problems raised in these examples illustrate the complexities involved in balancing off costs and benefits between individuals and between present and future resource use. The conflicts could be resolved *efficiently* if property rights were all clearly allocated (for example, if the residential property owners had a property right to peace and quiet that could be sold to the owner of the gas station site, or the farmer could sell view rights to adjoining property owners), and there were no costs involved in negotiating the terms of transfer and enforcing them.

Or the conflicts could be resolved efficiently if some government agency could perfectly estimate the value of the peace and quiet to the homeowner and charge him for it and compensate the auto owner for his inconvenience. Or if the same agency could subsidize the farm owner for keeping the farm in agricultural production and offset the subsidy with charges for the environmental amenity provided and with borrowings to be repaid from the high rents that would accrue from agricultural production in the food-short future. Or if the agency could charge for the pollution resulting from the subdivision.

In all cases, it is assumed that the agency has no administrative or enforcement costs for its operation and has perfect knowledge of the true costs and benefits of individuals who have strong incentives to overstate the costs to them of others' actions and understate the benefits that accrue to them. These assumptions are not realistic.

The examples illustrate the complexity of the efficiency criterion for land-use control institutions and procedures. Well-defined private property rights result in the internalization of costs and benefits so that individual's choices closely reflect the social costs and benefits of their choices. However, transaction and enforcement costs for individuals may be very high with consequent sufferance of nuisance costs from spillover effects.

Social control of the allocation of land uses could eliminate all transaction and enforcement costs for individuals but result in large administrative costs and enforcement costs for government agencies and the individuals who had to comply with their directives. And we assume that efficiency gains result from perfect knowledge by the government agencies of true costs and benefits!

To summarize, an efficient system for the control of land use should have the following characteristics: (1) It should allow land to be used for those activities that give the greatest present value of a discounted stream of net rents to all the land within a definable and vested political area. Property rights should be clearly defined and vested in order to minimize transaction and uncertainty costs that diminish net rents, as should administrative costs that necessitate financing by taxation that will also tend to diminish rents.

Equity

It is the nature of efficiency in resource management to allow all members of a society to be better off in absolute terms, and no one to be worse off. Equity, on the other hand, is concerned with the distribution of claims to the use of resources. Social controls over resource allocation inevitably increase the welfare of some members of society at the expense of others.

Equity necessitates decisions about entitlement. Who is entitled to use which land? Who is entitled to use the air, water, or oceans in which ways?

The efficiency criterion assumes some initial distribution of property rights in resource use and then asks whether any exchanges of rights can increase total welfare through Pareto-optimal exchanges. The equity criterion asks whether the existing distribution of property rights is fair ("equitable," "just") or could be changed to some new distribution that would be more equitable.

Any changes in the institutions that govern land use will have substantial effects on the distribution of property rights. I wish to avoid dealing with the issue of the equity or fairness of existing distributions of property rights. They have occurred by accepted legal processes, and their fairness depends on the fairness of those processes.

What I propose to do is to establish certain criteria for the process that *changes* the distribution of property rights. In this, I am following the principle laid down in the U.S. Constitution that allows the taking of private property for public use by due process and with just compensation.

The primary way in which society, through the agency of government, takes private property is through taxation. We have always operated under the premise that taxes were self-imposed on property holders (by their elected representatives). One of the principles on which taxation is based is equal treatment of equals. This has been translated into equal taxation for people of equal incomes. I would propose a similar criterion for the regulation of land use—that all landowners should be subject to similar taxation and regulations.

A second criterion under the equity heading is derived from the principle originally used to justify the alienation of land into private ownership—that it was just, fair, and equitable as long as the alienation did not deprive others and "as good and as plentiful" was left for others.[2] I derive from this principle that where this is *not* the case, the individual who uses resources should bear the cost or value of the use foregone by others.

This principle turns out to be the basis of our private property system. If I use land that is highly valued by others for my own use, I am forgoing the income that I could derive by selling the land or its use. It is where this principle does *not* presently operate that it should be extended. If I use the air as a pollution-dispersion medium and thereby impose costs on the rest of society, I am leaving myself richer and them poorer. The principle here is that the user of any resource should bear the full social cost of its use.

As discussed in chapter 4, there are different theories about the source of individual claims to property. The personality theory, which might be called "radical individualism" or "possessive individualism," emphasizes the source of property in human action. It starts with the premise that every individual has a right to liberty. The exercise of that liberty creates assets, and individuals safeguard these assets by mutual forbearance or contract or the creation of government to enforce contracts or mutual forbearance.

The other types of theory about individual claims to property base them in a corporate conception of society. Men are assumed to associate on the basis of need or desire and to allocate income and property in order to assure continuing support, cooperation, and incentives for production and abstention from consumption for individual members of the social group.

The moral basis of individual claims to land and natural resources for the radical individualist comes from the proviso that when there was original alienation of land, no one else was left worse off since there was plenty to go around. Subsequent claims to land occurred when men traded other wealth, legitimately acquired, perhaps by labor, for claims to land. If the original claims were just and the exchange transactions that produced the existing distribution of property rights were just, then the existing pattern of claims must be just. Men are entitled to what they own. Society does not create a pattern of distribution of ownership of assets. Individuals create it and are entitled to it.[3]

The weak link in the argument is the proviso that individual alienation leaves no other member of society worse off. If part of society has all the land, others are excluded, and if land produces an economic rent, it accrues to certain owners when it could as easily go to others.

The corporate conception of society finds the principles guiding the definition and distribution of property rights in collective agreements to maximize the enjoyment of total income subject to safeguards for the security and freedom of individuals. Property rights have their origins in society rather than the individual and are constantly undergoing redefinition in response to underlying principles agreed to be necessary for the successful functioning of the social group.

One recent formulation of this conception by John Rawls argues that the only principle that would be agreed to by men in an original contract specifying the form of future rules governing income distribution would be a "difference principle."[4] The difference principle would allow inequality only to the extent that it increased the absolute income of the least advantaged members of the society. The necessity of incentives to secure labor effort and capital accumulation is recognized, but the individual is not allowed to keep all his "own" production (however that happens to be measured and allocated). He is allowed to retain a differential only to the extent that this increases the absolute income of the least advantaged member of his society.

The corporate conception of society implies an equity rule with respect to returns from land and other natural resources. Insofar as income accrues to society from the sale of rights to use air and water and other natural resources, that income should be distributed to accord with the difference principle. Further, if site rent accrues to the owner of natural resources such as land, petroleum, coal, forests, places of natural or historic interest, those rents should be available for redistribution in accordance with the difference principle.

While the radical individualist and corporate conceptions of equity or entitlement have different implications with regard to property rights to income from labor or capital, they have similar implications with regard to property rights in land and natural resources. In neither case is there an equitable basis for individual entitlement to property rights in natural resources. There is a utilitarian basis for their recognition to secure efficient allocation and management to minimize transactions and enforcement costs.

A fundamental premise of an equity criterion for the evaluation of changes in the existing pattern of land-use control arises from the interdependence of social activities and resource uses. Many uses of land by one human will preclude its use by another. Many uses of air or water will diminish its quality in a way that imposes costs on others. The Lockean proviso that private alienation of land from collective possession is just as long as there is "as much and as good left for others" cannot be met in our society for land. It is increasingly inapplicable to air and water.

The equity criterion for any resource-control system must therefore ask whether the resource user pays the social cost of using the resource. It must also ask whether the rents that accrue from resource use are redistributed to society in accordance with the difference principle mentioned earlier.

The recognition of the principle of social cost and application of the difference principle to the distribution of economic rents from natural resources has far-reaching implications for the nature of private property in land and other natural resources. If the individual is constrained in his use of resources not to impose uncompensated costs on others and has no right to incomes from natural resources, what happens to "life, liberty, and property"?

The next chapter will argue that the application of the equity principles will make a substantial redistribution of the patterns of costs and incomes from resource use but need not do so in an arbitrary way and can do so with the maintenance of procedural safeguards against the arbitrary coercion of the individual by other individuals or the state.

Social Objectives

Any consistent set of policies controlling land use must have a well-defined set of objectives. Well-defined objectives are necessary because using land for one purpose precludes its use for another purpose. Vesting the control of land with one person precludes the use of it by others. There must be principles to guide the choices that are made.

These choices have not been difficult for the United States in the past because there was a relative abundance of land. The increasing scarcity of land—relative to the population, income, preferential and technologically based demands for land—and scarcity relative to capital and labor make it increasingly important to make careful choices.

What objectives have guided the assignment of property rights in the past? What objectives do we want to determine the form and definition of property rights and other determinants of land use in the future?

The objectives can be discussed under three separate headings—ethical, political, and economic. The objectives must be based on our conception of man and a just society and efficient means of facilitating individual choices.

Ethical objectives have been based on a conception of man. The western conception of man has emphasized the rationality of man and his responsibility for making choices. Man's transcendence over nature has stressed his power to control the physical and biological world for his own purposes. Man's relationship with other men has emphasized mutual forbearance in actions against the person or possessions of others based on the integrity of persons and every man's right to freedom from coercion by others.

The freedom of the individual to make choices about his own actions and his responsibility for those choices has been the ethical basis of individual property. Since man had a moral right to choose how he would use his time and energy, he had a moral right to what he produced. If a man chose to abstain from present consumption to produce capital goods, the capital was the result of his choices, and he had a moral right to it.

The argument always became more difficult when applied to land or natural resources since they were not created by man's exercise of his freedom. Locke claimed that man had a moral right to property in land if he had "mixed his labor with it" but, as we have noted (chapter 4), the elaboration of his arguments sometimes stressed beneficial use as long as every other member of the society had the same opportunity and sometimes stressed the utility to society of individual ownership when that increased total output.

There has always been a tension in western thought between the rights of the individual and his responsibilities to society. Both Christian and Judaic ethical systems have grappled with the extent of man's responsibilities for the welfare of his fellow man. This has manifested itself in differences of opinion about the ethical basis of man's claim to personal possession of assets.

The political basis of private property in land, like the ethical view, has been based on the concept of man. A dominant theme in western political thought has been the primacy of the individual. Social arrangements such as the state have been regarded as *agencies* created to foster and protect the preexisting rights of individuals. The function of the state has been seen as the provision of public goods such as defense and justice, "to provide," as Lincoln said, "those things which private citizens cannot do as cheaply or as well for themselves." Emphatically, the state was not to interfere with the distribution of income and wealth since that distribution arose from individual choices about how they would exercise their freedom. The absolute sanctity of private property from state control was a bulwark of freedom for the individual. How could a citizen have political freedom or individual security if the state could deprive him of his property for opposing the government or a majority opinion?

The economic objectives of property have already been discussed thoroughly in chapter 3. By internalizing costs and benefits, property assures that individual choices about asset use will reflect social valuations of the costs and benefits of using property. It is assumed to provide the incentives for development and efficient management. Private property is assumed to have lower enforcement and administrative costs than alternative systems for asset management. The use of private property to control land use is premised on a concept of man driven by economic self-interest and able to make rational choices that will maximize his own well-being and, thereby, the well-being of others.

How well do the objectives and concepts of man and society that have molded our definitions of property rights and policies affecting land use in the past fit the present and the future? I would suggest that there are differences in our concepts and problems that necessitate some restatement of objectives.

The first area in which this is true is ethics. Our concept of man has been undergoing a change. Man is no longer seen as an independent agent making choices in isolation. Man sees himself as part of an ongoing human history in which his present position depends to a large extent on what his ancestors have done in the use of their freedom and in their use of the natural world. From this comes an ethical concern for the world that he will pass on to others. In a world in which land is increasingly scarce, individuals are coming to recognize that their use of land does leave less for others. The exclusive possession and control of land that property vests in one person does limit the freedom of others. The protection of the freedom of one individual to exercise choice can no longer be an ethical absolute because of the limitations it places on the freedom of others.

In the political sphere, the responsibility of the state for accomplishing redistribution of property rights to income is increasingly acknowledged. The formulation of the ethical basis for this comes from work such as that of John Rawls. Rawls argues that the only principles for control of human activity that could be called just are those that rational, self-interested individuals would settle on in the original organization of society behind a "veil of ignorance."[5] He argues that behind this "veil of ignorance" as to their future place in society or knowledge of their own endowment of mental and physical powers they would settle on several principles. One principle is equality of opportunity and access to all the privileges offered by that society to its members. The other is the "difference principle" that postulates that inequalities of wealth or income will be admissible only to the extent that they work to the advantage of the least advantaged members of the society.

Rawls applies this principle even to the income that accrues to the individual from the superiority of, say, natural intelligence. The inventor whose ideas enrich him can retain his supernormal income only to the point where its further redistribution would so limit his incentives that he would limit his efforts and their limitation would leave less for redistribution.

The implications of this concept of social arrangements for the distribution of the economic rents that accrue from land or natural resources (as well as the rents to superior ability that accrue to athletes, musicians, or scientists) is obvious. They should be redistributed. Sufficient income should be retained by the owners of assets to provide an inducement for their improvement and efficient allocation, management and conservation, and the rest should be taxed away by the state for redistribution. This idea can also be found in the writings of Henry George.[6]

It is in the area of economic objectives that we have the greatest need for close examination. In the past the internalization of benefits from the development of forest or prairie to farm or the conversion of agricultural to residential or residential to industrial use accorded with social needs for food, housing, and manufactured goods. A forest might have provided small aesthetic benefits and watershed benefits in the past, but they were outweighed by the social priority put on cheap lumber for housing. Not using open spaces near cities for agricultural or residential development would have necessitated the use of more capital or labor for transportation. Now there may be great public benefit derived from the proximity of open spaces or natural areas in or near urban areas. But private owners cannot easily internalize the benefits, and they have a strong incentive to develop them so they can. Thus our institutions may no longer accord even with our economic objectives and criteria for economic efficiency.

Notes

1. Readers interested in a more extensive analysis of the problem of risk and uncertainty in private versus public decisions affecting resource utilization and conservation should see Kenneth Arrow and Robert Lind, "Uncertainty and the Evaluation of Public Investment Decisions," *American Economic Review* 60 (1978); Anthony Fisher and John Krutilla, "Resource Conservation, Environmental Preservation and the Rate of Discount," *Quarterly Journal of Economics* 89 (1975).

2. This is the famous "Lockean Proviso." For a discussion, see Robert Nozick, *Anarchy, State and Utopia* (New York: Basic Books, 1974), pp. 175ff., and G.C. Bjork, *Private Enterprise and Public Interest: The Development of American Capitalism* (Englewood Cliffs, N.J.: Prentice-Hall, 1969), chapters 3,4,5.

3. This argument forms the basis of the libertarian argument developed by Nozick, *Anarchy, State and Utopia,* pp. 149ff.

4. John Rawls, *A Theory of Justice* (Cambridge, Mass.: Belknap Press of Harvard University Press, 1971).

5. Ibid., pp. 136ff.

6. Henry George, *Progress and Poverty* (New York, 1883; Modern Library Edition, 1940).

The Control of Land and Environmental Amenity: Some Proposals

Institutional arrangements to control the use of land, water, or the environment cannot affect the total quantity of resources available. They can only change the distribution and efficiency of the uses that are made of the resources as they alter human behavior. This is the intent and effect of the social institutions that structure and determine resource use.

The primary purpose of the changes in institutional arrangements that this chapter proposes is to make individuals, corporations, and government officials consider the real costs of using resources. If institutions force individuals to bear the real cost of resource use, we can secure use patterns that are both more efficient and more equitable.

Some land-use choices, like ownership of a residence, can be made by an individual on the basis of a market price. This price represents what buyers generally consider to be its value relative to alternatives. This price of course depends on a multitude of politically determined factors such as taxation, zoning, and the pricing of public utility services that affect the costs and benefits of owning and using a particular parcel of land.

Other land-use choices like the siting of a freeway or the maintenance of a coastal park, are not subject to individual choices but must be made by governmental agencies that, it is hoped, allocate taxpayer money in line with what are determined to be taxpayer priorities. These choices, as individual choices, should be made on the basis of real costs.

Because land is becoming more and more scarce, the choices that must be made between alternative land uses will become more and more expensive: using land for a park rather than a housing tract is more expensive than using land for a park instead of agriculture because the market value of the land uses that must be forgone is greater. As land becomes more expensive, pressures will mount to have government agencies pay the increasing costs and redistribute them via the tax mechanism. Or land-use regulations that place the costs on individual landowners will be used to conceal the costs.

If the government zones a piece of seacoast for open space and deprives the erstwhile owner and other potential owners of its development potential, it effectively makes the owner forgo a valuable use and allows the public to escape payment for a valuable use forgone.

As land prices rise, the individual owner may deduct from his taxable income interest on his mortgage and property taxes on his real estate without having to impute any income on his tax return for the value of services enjoyed. This allows him to shift part of the cost of land ownership onto other taxpayers.

It is inefficient and inequitable to have land-use decisions made within frameworks that distort the patterns of real costs. It should be a basic principle of equity and efficiency that choices about the use of land should be made on the basis of real costs, and the person who derives the benefit from a particular use of a parcel of land should, insofar as possible, bear the cost of that use. All the policy recommendations that follow in this chapter are based on that principle.

Public Ownership of Environmental Quality

The first proposal to assure the efficient and equitable use of land and other natural resources is that public ownership of the ambient air, water, and soundwaves be affirmed and be made a basis for the regulation and control of all forms of pollution or diminution of the quality of the natural environment. This is in no sense a radical departure from the basic principles of property rights and social behavior that have informed our socioeconomic system in the past. The federal Constitution provides for the federal control of navigable waterways. In historical context this control could be interpreted as the public preemption of resource use where actions by an individual citizen could adversely affect the welfare of other citizens.

The constitutions of several states explicitly provide that the waters of the state are public property and that the use thereof will be regulated by appropriate systems of law. The common-law treatment of nuisances has always made air or noise pollution a matter for equitable resolution by the courts. The fact of temporal priority in the use of the air or environment for uses that impose costs on later users has never been an adequate defense in court decisions.[1]

The public ownership of natural resources of air and water implies that a charge should be collected for any use of those resources that diminishes the quality or quantity of those resources left for others. The conceptual character of this user charge is identical to the payment of a rent to the owner of land for the use of the land. Its social function is to assure that the opportunity cost of using a resource will be taken into account by the user. The user charge also provides an income to the owner (in this case, the public) that is based on socially recognized property rights. Elsewhere it was argued that the social distribution and allocation of rents that arise from social regulations and activities is a primary political function.[2]

For Madisonian reasons of dividing political power and for administrative efficiency, state governments should be designated as the responsible governmental units for the determination and collection of resource-use fees, and the income from use fees should be treated as a part of general revenue for the provision of general public services or the reduction of general taxation.

Because there are many instances in which the use of air or water raises issues that are intrastate (for example, southern California) or interregional (for example, the New York City metropolitan area or the Columbia River hydrologic system), it will be appropriate in many instances for state governments to delegate responsibility to other governmental units as is done presently when state governments grant powers to incorporated areas.

The control principle here incorporates the two principles of efficiency and equity. A fee payment to the state government should be charged to any user of air or water who diminishes its quality or quantity. The fee should be based on the real costs to other members of society of using the air and water that is public property.

Real costs here appear in two guises — as reductions of satisfaction from reduction of air quality and water quality and quantity directly and in terms of depriving the public of other goods or increasing their costs. Several clarifying examples are in order.

Air pollution may cause a reduction in the standard of living by its effects on health or enjoyment of the environment. It may peel paint, soil fabric, or necessitate the use of air-conditioners that have both capital and operating costs. The control of air pollution also has costs: controlling the exhaust emission from automobiles may increase the purchase price of automobiles and lessen gas mileage or engine life. Controlling the emission from a power plant may necessitate large additional capital costs and/or more expensive fuel or other operating costs.

Controlling noise pollution, the pollution of the airwaves, may entail heavy capital expenditures by the noise producer (silencing devices or physical removal) or similar actions by those who suffer from the noise.

There is a given annual flow of water in any hydrologic system. It can be diminished in quantity by uses that increase its evaporation or transpiration (such as agriculture) or its quality by use as a dissipator of waste. In addition to an annual flow of water, there is a capital stock of water in a hydrologic basin. Most of the capital stock is the result of natural recharge of lakes or underground water-bearing strata (aquifers). Some is man-made by the creation of dams (which do no more than even out the seasonal flow of water to make it more available when needed).

The real cost of water to society is the value of goods and services forgone by the use of water for a particular use or the diminution of satisfactions resulting from the use of water for a particular use. If a stream is used for the dissipation of sewage, there are social savings from not having to operate sewage-treatment facilities. On the other hand, the public may lose the recreational value of the stream for swimming and fishing and downstream users may have to install expensive water-treatment facilities in order to use the water.

Maintaining summer stream flow in a river in order to permit navigation by vessels of a certain draft may require that irrigation, which could provide valuable foodstuffs, must be forgone. Or pumping groundwater today to produce hay of little value may reduce the natural capital stock of groundwater available for raising tomatoes in the future except at higher costs.

The reason for asserting public ownership of air, water, and solitude is *not* to prevent pollution or use of groundwater or to prevent noise but to ensure that the use of natural resources does not impose costs on some citizens that are larger than the benefits realized by the user.

There is a great deal of confusion in the public discussion of protection of the environment. Most of the discussion of pollution proceeds on the implicit assumption that pollution is in wanton disregard of the rights of the public and that fines ought to be imposed on polluters like those imposed on traffic violators. The federal Environmental Protection Agency, for example, has suggested imposing fines on industrial polluters equal to the cost of pollution-control equipment. This approach recognizes that the control of pollution has costs that makes polluters loath to stop doing it. It fails to recognize that it is the costs that pollution imposes on the public that need to be equated with the charge or fine rather than with the costs of pollution-control equipment.

Suppose, for example, that a power plant located in the middle of the desert imposed only minimal reduction in air quality for the surrounding sparse population but that the costs of mitigating the pollution were very large compared to the benefits of slightly cleaner air to a small number of adjoining residents. It would be very wasteful, from a social point of view, to establish air-quality regulations that required the operators of the power plant to spend large sums for pollution control because the benefits would be minimal.

Should the affected residents be compensated individually for the effects of pollution? I would argue not on the grounds that their enjoyment of clean air is the use of a public good to which they have no property rights as *individuals*. The power plant has taken some of the air quality that they formerly enjoyed without payment to the public because they did not diminish its quality or quantity in a way that imposed costs on others. If the use of the air as a pollution disperser is now "sold" via user charges to the power plant, the neighbors of the power plant have no specific claim on the income from the fees as the air quality was not their specific property. They share in the user fees only as citizens.

Consider the alternative solution to the conflict between individuals with conflicts over rights to the enjoyment of air, water, or solitude. People could move to land adjacent to an airport and claim compensation from the airport for the noise. They would in effect be receiving income from airport users for the airport users' use of public property. Awarding compensation to those who are affected by the diminution of air quality, water quantity or quality, or silence implicitly grants them *individual* property rights in the use of these resources. So do zoning or systems of riparian rights that give privileged access to natural resources to *particular citizens.*

The recognition of public property in air, water, and solitude is asserted to ensure the efficient and equitable management of those resources. The appropriate way to exercise this management is by user fees rather than limitations or standards.

Consider a hypothetical example to make clear the superiority of fees to standards in the case of conflicting claims to water use: Suppose that the state of New York passes a law requiring all sewage-treatment plants emptying into the Hudson to meet an extremely high standard of purity. Suppose that the costs of this treatment are very high for the citizens of Troy, but the benefits of these extremely high standards of water purity to downstream users are substantially less. Consider the following table:

Cost Trade-offs for the Use of a Natural Resource to Society

Pollution (Physical Index)	Cost of Reducing Pollution to Given Level (to City of Troy)	Costs of Pollution to Downstream Users (New York City)
0	$20,000	0
100	10,000	500
200	5,000	1,000
300	3,000	2,000
400	2,100	3,200
500	1,200	4,500
600	800	6,500
700	500	9,000
800	250	12,000
900	0	20,000

Consider the alternatives open to New York State:

1. Do nothing to control pollution.
2. Establish a high standard for water quality that virtually eliminates pollution.
3. Establish a set of charges for use of the Hudson to disperse pollution based on estimated costs to downstream users.

Alternative 1 would be inefficient. Even a minimal expenditure of $250 could reduce the costs of pollution by $8000. (Going from pollution level 900 to 800 costs Troy $250 and benefits New York City $8000.) Alternative 2 would also be inefficient. Moving from a pollution index of 100 to 0 costs Troy $10,000 and saves New York City only $500. Alternative 3 would set pollution charges equal to the costs to downstream users. Troy would decide, under the circumstances, to operate at a pollution index of 300 where they would pay a charge of $2000 to the state of New York. They would not opt to reduce the pollution index to 200 where the user charge would be $1000 ($1000 less) because the cost of doing so would increase by $2000. They would not opt to increase the pollution index to 400 because this would reduce their costs by only $900 while it increases their user charges by $1200.

Careful inspection of the table will demonstrate that there is no way to reduce the combined total costs of both pollution-control equipment and losses to downstream users to a lower level than is achieved at a pollution index of 300.

Several other questions might be asked. Why not have the state of New York set a standard or regulation for water purity at an index of 300 but not impose any charge? This would enrich the citizens of Troy (who are using state property) at the expense of the citizens of New York State as a whole.

Why not impose the charge on Troy but then give it to New York City as compensation for the pollution damages? This would implicitly allow the citizens of New York City to use the Hudson at the expense of the citizens of New York State.

Any solution that allows the citizens of Troy or New York City to use the Hudson without charge gives them property rights in a stream of benefits (or forgone costs) that, I would argue, ought to belong to the citizens of New York State as a whole.

The principle of social cost is at issue in the implicit conflict between the citizens of Troy and the citizens of New York City over the use of the Hudson River. Assuming all the hypothetical conditions necessary for private parties to reach a maximum benefit solution in a conflict over rights (no transaction costs, perfect information), a final bargain would be struck (in our example) at a pollution index of 300. If Troy had property rights in the Hudson that allowed it to pollute, New York City would pay a bribe to Troy of $2000 to contain pollution to the 300 index. If New York City had property rights in the Hudson, it would accept a payment from Troy of $2000 to pollute up to the 300 level.

The principle of state ownership (rather than making either city the burdened party) is based on the reality (assumed away in the example) that the use of natural resources affects all the citizens of a geographic area rather than the residents of a few, easily isolated subdivisions.

The designation of state governments as the administrative units for the public ownership and control of air and water is inevitably arbitrary because hydrologic and air basins do not coincide with state lines. It might be appropriate to set up interstate authorities for air in areas like New York City or intrastate regional authorities for areas like southern California or the San Francisco Bay area.

The logic of establishing state rather than federal control of resources such as air and water stems from the differential scarcity and social costs of using those resources in different parts of the country. Mississippi might decide, for example, that the marginal social costs of using water and air for the dispersion of wastes were quite low while Connecticut might consider them to be quite high. Mississippi might therefore attract industries with high pollution-control costs to relocate from Connecticut.

The control of water will become an increasingly more difficult political issue as competing demands for this scarce resource mount. Where hydrologic basins are interstate in character, it may be necessary to assign state quotas for annual withdrawals. (There are already arrangements of this sort on the Columbia and the Colorado.) These quotas could then be sold by one state to another state where there were higher value uses. Thus if it were much more valuable to use Colorado River water for lettuce in California than for alfalfa in Colorado, Colorado could sell some of its water to California, which could in turn sell it to the lettuce growers. Coloradans would have higher incomes from the payments by California, and California would have higher incomes from the increased lettuce production.

If air and water are to be treated as public property and a fee is to be charged for their use, then it is appropriate that the income from the use of the public property be available for expenditure (or reduction of taxes) in line with the choices of individual citizens of the states as expressed and resolved by their elected representatives. The fees charged for using the air as a pollution sink by Alabama are a compensation paid to the citizens of that state for the social costs that they bear as a result of that use of their public resource. If the citizens of Alabama decide that the air capacity for pollution dispersion in Alabama is so underutilized relative to other states that they could charge a fee for its use somewhat above their real social costs to increase their revenues and reduce their taxes, more power to them. Air should be considered as a resource just as cheap available industrial sites should be.

If southern California decides that the reduction of pollution is a very important objective because of its high social costs, it is economically rational to impose higher fees than other states for emission of pollutants. One implication of this policy decision is that southern California should add a pollution-control tax to gasoline that will increase the costs of motoring to the individual and compensate the general public for the costs imposed on them by the motorists' decisions. Or California could tax vehicles on the basis of their estimated pollution. California's present approach of requiring more stringent pollution-control equipment runs the risk of being inefficient. The capital and operating costs of the pollution-control equipment may have higher costs than benefits, or additional benefits might be secured with less than proportional expenditures.

There is an important distinction to be made between a designated-use tax such as the gasoline tax, which represents a payment for the use of roads and is properly designated for their construction and maintenance, and a pollution tax or fee, which is imposed to force polluters to take into account their use of a public resource and to compensate the public for their costs of pollution. The former is a payment for service to a public producer of services while the latter is a payment for resource use to the public that bears the cost of resource use.

The determination of appropriate levels of fees for the use of public resources such as air and water is a task well within the competence of the legislature with the assistance of professional staff to estimate the economic magnitudes involved. What bears emphasis here is the *conceptual* importance to ensure efficient use of asserting public ownership of what have heretofore been viewed as open access resources with no property rights. It is this conceptual change for which I am arguing.[3]

The establishment of public property rights in air and water meets our criteria for efficiency and equity. The user of the resource who imposes costs on others is forced to internalize the costs and balance them against the benefits. While it would theoretically be possible for the public at large to compensate users of air and water for not using the resources (that is, make the public at large the burdened party), this practice would be less efficient from an administrative point of view because of the large number of diffuse interests.

The equity of the solution is to be found in leaving property rights to resource use with those whose use does not diminish the resources in question.

Reduction of Zoning Powers

The second proposal is closely related to the first even though it may appear at first glance to be diametrically opposed from a conceptual or public policy vantage point. The rights of private property in land should be affirmed.

Individual owners should be secure in their rights to determine the highest and best use for their land. Where there are external costs and benefits to land use, they should be resolved, insofar as possible, by private negotiation. Public agencies should take an active role in acquiring land and rights to limited public uses of private land, but this acquisition should be accomplished by negotiation or use restriction or condemnation with compensation.

Restrictions on the permitted uses of land by zoning interferes with the owner's determination of highest and best uses. The use of zoning powers by local government or state governments should be rescinded by state legislatures. Public health and safety can be protected adequately by statewide standards for such things as prohibitions on building in unsafe areas such as flood plains or earthquake sites, requirements that adequate water and sewage-disposal facilities are used, fire-resistant construction and fire-access are ensured. Such matters as air and noise pollution and water use are covered under the first recommendation for public affirmation of ownership and control of these scarce openaccess resources.

The positive case for zoning, for private ownership of land, and the allocation of land use by the market have been discussed. Zoning does have a *potentially* positive role to play in the reduction of external costs, the provision of environmental amenities, and the reduction of transaction costs. Alas, its use is all too frequently to thwart individual choices about efficient land use, promote the wasteful use of land, and force the private provision of environmental public amenities without payment by those who benefit from restrictions on land use.

There is a powerful economic incentive for individuals to get everyone else's land zoned for less intensive use and their own for more intensive use. There is a powerful economic incentive for towns to zone out low-income residents. There is a powerful economic incentive for individuals to secure regulation of land use that will allow them to avoid costs or secure benefits at the expense of their neighbors. There is a powerful incentive to use zoning to secure, by political means, the use of property rights without paying for them. The use of zoning satisfies neither our criterion of efficiency nor equity. By concealing real costs and reallocating them by the political process, zoning is a major cause of wasteful use of land.

Zoning land for open space when there is a great demand for its residential use deprives families of choice about where they would live and be willing to pay the cost. It forces them to pay more for a site they would value less. If the public wants the environmental amenity of open spaces, let them pay for it by purchase of a scenic easement, or development rights, or freehold ownership, rather than taking these rights from the existing owner by zoning without compensation. The social cost of preserving open spaces for public use is the satisfaction lost by families who wanted them for residential use. They are forced to pay higher prices for less satisfaction elsewhere.

A community that zones land for large lots or forces the use of large lots by a variety of building code limitations on heights, setbacks, or house/lot size ratios may increase the amenities of space. But if this space were really highly valued, land developers would take note of public preferences and subdivide into larger lots with covenants on land use that would maximize the value to prospective owners. A community only zones restrictions when people's natural maximizing behavior would result in another more highly valued use (or when high transaction costs would preclude them from doing so by negotiation). Once again the losers are the potential members of the community excluded by the legal requirement of buying more land than they can afford.

Zoning does not meet the criterion of institutions that foster Pareto-optimal adjustment of interests. It is inequitable because of its arbitrary and random redistribution of benefits without reference to the real costs of particular land uses. Its purposes can be accomplished better by other governmental policies and private actions.

Positive Governmental Land-Use Policies

The third proposal is to increase the role of government in explicit and indicative planning for future land use. There is a positive role for all levels of government in land-use planning. This positive role is to make explicit decisions about which land shall be used for the provision of public goods. Starting with agriculture, explicit planning policies need to be instituted at the federal level to estimate demand for food and wood products and the derived demand for land for twenty-five or fifty years into the future based on population projections and alternative agricultural technologies.

One of the important unknowns is world demand for food and fiber based on U.S. export policies. This variable in turn depends on foreign-policy decisions. Shall international trade and specialization of labor be encouraged? If Japan buys our food exports, we will have to buy their color-television sets and automobiles. If India buys our food, it will probably have to be with money the United States "loans" to India. Does the United States want to trade with Russia? Wheat for oil and natural gas?

Questions about agricultural technology are intimately linked to a national energy policy. United States agriculture is presently very energy intensive. The amount of land needed for agriculture and silviculture in the future will depend on the prices of fuel for soil preparation and fertilization produced from petrochemicals and natural gas.

Agricultural production will be affected by future federal policies with respect to land reclamation. Dams and irrigation systems have enormously increased agricultural production in the past. The amount of land needed in the future depends to a large extent on federal decisions about capital expenditures for dams and irrigation and control of rivers.

When the federal government has made the necessary projections and policy decisions, it will be possible to develop some estimates of the demand for agricultural land in the future. *If* it develops that the United States, for a variety of reasons connected with choices about foreign policy, energy policy, federal water projects, and so on, estimates that the demand for land will be greater in the future, *then* the federal government can take steps to ensure its availability.

Agricultural land cannot be allowed to stand idle. If it will be needed in the future but is not needed now, the federal government will have to create a system of economic incentives to keep it readily available for agricultural production or purchase it outright and lease it back to farmers or hire them to maintain it in "soil banks" or some such program.

Once the projections about future agricultural land needs have been made on the basis of a variety of policy decisions and projections, alternative land-use control mechanisms to preserve agricultural land can be developed. They would be made, it is hoped, on a cost-benefit basis.

What does not make sense, from a planning point of view, is to have counties or states make decisions based on incomplete knowledge or uninformed judgments that certain parcels of land should be preserved for future agricultural use when the market mechanism would presently value them much more highly for some other use.

There are other reasons why people may wish to protect and preserve agricultural land. It may provide visual amenities for nearby city dwellers or reduce public expenditures by preventing sprawl. European agriculture has been deliberately maintained at high cost by subsidies and tariffs and support prices to preserve countryside, provide a food supply in the case of national emergency, and provide electoral support for agrarian-based parties. But if these are the policy objectives of the United States, they should be explicitly recognized for what they are.

A second area in which explicit governmental choices need to be made is in the provision of parks and the preservation of areas of scenic beauty or historic interest. In the western United States, large areas of land are owned by the federal government and administered by the Bureau of Land Management of the Interior Department or the Forest Service of the Agriculture Department. Policies and appropriations to increase the recreational use of forest or rangeland or desert can easily be effected by the Congress although there will be conflicts here with the alternative uses of these lands for grazing and lumbering.

In the eastern United States, much less land is in public ownership, and the provision of recreational opportunities will necessitate the purchase of access rights or scenic easements or other explicit expenditures to provide public-access facilities and administration of recreational facilities. Suffolk County, New York, has recently demonstrated one approach to this objective by purchasing the development rights to land and financing the pur chase with bond issues.

A primary thrust of these policy recommendations is that public decisions to provide public recreation and environmental amenities should be accomplished by explicit purchase or subsidy rather than by placing restrictions on uses that force the private provision of public goods by a taking of property rights without compensation. Once again the operative principle is that explicit choices should be made on the basis of real costs.

States and local governments have very substantial impact on land-use patterns by their siting of streets, sewers, power plants, schools and colleges, prisons and hospitals, and state offices. State and local governments are in a unique position to consider the overall impact of their actions rather than the narrow considerations of land cost and related costs that form a basis for private land-use decisions. A requirement for comprehensive analysis of benefits and costs should be required for all governmentally funded projects.

What considerations other than monument building prompted New York City to build the World Trade Center in the already congested Wall Street area? The decision further increased commuter congestion in Lower Manhattan and allowed the continuing deterioration of northern Manhattan and the Bronx. City and state offices have been quartered in the building rather than in other districts where their presence would have had less dramatic impact on traffic congestion and more favorable impact on neighborhoods that were declining because of inadequate economic bases. One might equally question the economic rationality of rebuilding the West Side Highway in Manhattan at a cost of over a billion dollars when it can only contribute to further traffic congestion on Manhattan.

Cities and states are in a unique position in siting decisions to take into account benefits and costs that would be external to the maximizing decisions of a private developer. The operative rule for decision making should be to site a facility where it will have the greatest benefit-cost ratio of all the alternatives available.

As an example, a city or state siting a new college should take into consideration land cost plus the cost of public services such as roads, sewers, and so on, plus the probable commutation expenses for students and staff. On the benefit side, the value placed by the community on access to the college should be compared. The total benefit-cost approach has been required for three decades on federally funded reclamation projects. It has been used — and misused — but its overall impact has certainly aided in the selection of alternatives that were superior to straightforward congressional or administrative control based purely on "pork-barrel" politics.

Tax Changes and Land-Use Decisions

The fourth set of proposals center on taxation. Their purpose is to promote the more intensive use of land by differential taxation of land and improvements to land. A related purpose is to equalize the after-tax cost of land ownership and land use to individuals in different taxable-income brackets.

The present pattern of taxes imposed by federal, state, and local governments on individuals and corporations is complex and pervasive in its effects on resource allocation and income distribution. This discussion cannot provide a comprehensive critique or set of proposals for tax reform, but it will indicate some ways in which modifications to the tax system would result in more efficient and equitable use of land.[4]

There are features of the present tax system that violate the principles of equity and efficiency in land use. First, an individual or corporation pays no tax on the implicit or imputed income from land ownership, and, second, because property taxes are deductible from taxable income, high-income individuals pay a lower percentage of their income or the value of their property in local property taxes.

As discussed in chapter 6, the present system of income taxation and local property taxation subsidizes the ownership of land by individuals. The higher a person's income, the greater the subsidy. This practice violates the first criterion of efficiency because the subsidy reduces the real cost of land use to the owner. It also violates the principle of equity since people with different after-tax incomes pay different amounts for the use of land after tax deductions. There are several ways to deal with the problem:

1.   The imputed value of income from land should be treated as a part of gross income for tax purposes and should be taxed at the same rate as other income for both individuals and corporations.
2.   Local taxes for resident homeowners should be based on income rather than the assessed value of real property. They should be levied as a percent of federal tax liability and should not be treated as a deduction from the federal tax return.
3.   A tax on the imputed income from land owned by nonresident individuals and corporations should be levied by local governments on the basis of the corporate tax rate. Corporations or nonresident individuals owning land within a local government jurisdiction should be taxed on the basis of the corporate tax liability for land within the local government area, but this should be treated as an expense in the calculation of net income for corporate tax purposes.

The imputation of income from land ownership could be accomplished easily within our present administrative framework for tax assessment. Local government units presently assess real property for tax purposes. Most differentiate between land value and buildings. The assessments established by present city or county tax assessors could be used as a basis for the evaluation of the current market value of land.

The imputed income from land should be taken as the market rate of return on the capital value of the land (since the capital value of land is estimated by the formula $C = R/i$, where C is capital value, R is annual net income, and i is the interest rate, $R = C \times i$). This rate could be established arbitrarily from time to time at an appropriate even figure for ease in tax calculations. The average rate of return on long-term government bonds would comfortably understate the real return on land because of the greater liquidity and lower risk on bonds.

What would be the effect on the price of land and its use of taxing the imputed income from land at the same rate as other income? The use of land would become more expensive for individuals with high incomes and for corporations, and they would use less of it and use it more intensively. The net rents on land (see chapter 6) would tend to fall and so would the market value.

What would be the likely effects of the change in tax structure on the behavior of the individual allocating his income and wealth between the purchase of land and other goods? The ownership of land would become more expensive because of the tax liability for imputed income from land ownership. On the other hand, since the imputed value from buildings would not be taxed as a part of income and the capital value of buildings would no longer be the basis for the assessment of local property taxes, there would be an incentive to increase investment in buildings. The homeowner would have an incentive to build a nicer house on a smaller lot. The factory owner would have an incentive to build a two-story factory on a lot half the size and to offer incentives to his employees to use mass transit or shared rides to lessen his expenditures for parking areas. The farmer would have an incentive to use more capital on a smaller area of land.

A presumption underlying these proposals is that local property taxation ought to be based on the income of residents rather than their ownership of real estate. Public support of this position can be inferred by the enormous support for the "Jarvis Amendment," Proposition 13, in California in 1978. Local taxes based on the assessed value of property originated in the nineteenth century when income taxes levied by federal government were prohibited by the Constitution and when the concept of an annual income was not as widespread as presently. A person's ownership of real property was generally regarded as a reasonable indicator of his ability to pay. Further, property taxes were initially levied for the provision of streets and roads and fire and police protection, and there was a rough correspondence between the value of these services to the individual and his ownership of real property.

Local government expenditures have expanded to include schools, hospitals, libraries, and welfare programs. Ownership of real property is no longer an adequate measure of income because of the importance of other forms of assets. Nor is the value of the services produced by local government proportional to the ownership of real property. This is why federal revenue sharing is an increasingly important element of local government finance.

The problem with federal revenue sharing is that there is no direct link between the cost of services provided by the local government unit and the tax liability of their residents. There is no means of balancing benefits and costs.[5] This creates an incentive for local governments to shift the burden for providing services to the federal government, and it has been a growing contributor to the deficit position of the federal budget.

One of the side-effects of the proposal would be the improvement of information for the taxpayer about the relative efficiency of his local government and protection against its confiscation of the value of his property by taxation.

Accountability for fiscal actions by local and state governments would increase as taxes were based on federal income-tax liability rather than local property assessments. People are mobile between tax jurisdictions. Real estate is not.

When property taxes rise in New York City because city politicians increase the number of municipal employees and their wages and fringe benefits, the owner of New York real estate suffers a reduction in his income and the capital value of his property. His income and wealth is redistributed, and his alternatives are limited to "voting the rascals out" and hoping that a new lot does not take their place.

If New York City (and state) base their tax demands on incomes, however, there is constraint on their tax demands from the competition of other cities and states for resident taxpayers. If taxpayer Smith decides that his tax rates based on federal tax liability of 20 percent for New York City and 20 percent for New York State compare unfavorably with 10 percent for Newark and 10 percent for New Jersey in terms of the public services and amenities enjoyed in both cities and states, he can move across the river. The knowledge that he can move forces cities and states to compete for the taxpayer on the basis of the highest value of public services per tax dollar of expenditure.

It may be objected that this policy will allow the affluent to flee the central cities for the suburbs to avoid taxes. And that is precisely true. It is what they have been doing in America for the last thirty years. Rising taxes and declining public services took place because corrupt and inefficient city governments could confiscate part of the real returns on fixed assets in urban real estate. But building maintenance suffered, and when tax liabilities consumed all the income flow from the properties, they were abandoned to the tax collector while new investment in real estate went to the suburbs.

If incomes had been taxed rather than property, the disparities between areas on the basis of tax rates versus values of public services would have been so apparent that voters would have taken immediate action to remedy the disparity. Why should cities, counties, and states not compete in terms of the services they provide and the taxes they collect?

What about the financing of schools, welfare, and medical services — items that take increasing proportions of local and state tax revenues? The fact that people are mobile probably argues for the federalization of finance for these types of income-redistributive categories of public expenditure.

The overassessment or underassessment of property poses a potential threat to the workability of the system. A local tax assessor might be pressured by the fiscal needs of his city to overassess the value of land owned by corporations or nonresident individuals. Underassessment also presents a problem since the person or corporation underassessed will never protest the low assessment, but a low assessment increases the tax rate or the assessment that will be imposed on others.

Assessment is a problem in the present system of property taxes. One way to control the equitable assessment of real property would be to provide that when an overassessment was protested, the land in question could be offered for sale at the assessed value. If there were no purchasers at that price, the landowner could demand purchase by the local tax authority at, say 110 percent of the assessed value. Underassessment could be minimized by the provision that assessed value was the basis for compensation when land was purchased by a public authority.

Two points should be borne in mind. Local property taxes are to be based on income rather than the value of real estate so the incentive for the local tax authority to over- or underestimate assessed value is diminished. Second, fair assessment becomes more important since income taxation of individuals now includes an imputation of income from the use of land.

It bears emphasis that the preceding proposals are not the resurrection of Henry George's "single tax" on the rental value of land. George wanted to confiscate all the site rent on land for purposes of income redistribution. The proposals here merely advocate the *taxation* of the imputed income from land at the same rate as other income and are coupled with the shifting of local government finance from the property tax to an income tax. The purpose of the proposals is to stop the present tax subsidy of land ownership that makes the cost of using land lower for high-income individuals than lower-income individuals and makes the use of land less expensive than the use of other assets because of tax treatment.

Marginal Cost Pricing for Public Utilities and Services

The final recommendation is that state utility commissions should require that public utilities provide services on a marginal cost basis to new users. The present system of utility pricing contributes to the abandonment or underutilization of the invested capital in existing sewer, water, electrical, and gas-distribution systems and the subsidization of new users by owners of existing sites.

Developers of residential or commercial sites are presently required by many planning authorities to provide streets and sidewalks. Some are even required to "donate" sites for schools or parks. This practice internalizes the costs of these facilities into the price of the house lots. This principle should be extended in the pricing of public utilities. Either the electric and gas companies should be required to charge a capital sum for the extension of service to an area to be incorporated into the prices of lots or users in the area should be charged with the incremental capital costs rather than their being incorporated into the capital investment on which rates are charged to all users of the utility.

The present system of utility pricing contributes to urban sprawl through the subsidization of capital costs for the development of new land by existing areas. It thus increases the cost of real estate ownership in existing areas and reduces it in new areas below its real costs. This subsidizes suburban sprawl and the decay of existing areas.

Summary

The United States does require a different institutional framework to guide land-use decisions. Land-use planning has come to mean proscriptive planning by governmental agencies for land use. The preceding analysis and proposals reject the notion that decisions about land use, and who shall benefit and who shall pay, are wisely left to government officials. The proposals have asserted a positive role for government in the establishment of an administrative framework that would, insofar as possible, lead to private choices about the best use of land based on knowledge of real costs for land-use choices and the bearing of those costs by those who benefit.

I personally share with many proponents of land-use controls a desire for more environmental amenities and a concern for the preservation of agricultural land and open spaces. I believe, however, that well-defined and enforced property rights are more likely to be a solution to the problem than their abridgement by various controls. I am more inclined to see existing governmental policies with respect to the pricing of public goods and public utilities, taxation, and zoning as causes of our present misuse of land.

My final rejoinder to those who would urge land-use planning by a statewide or federal extension of zoning is a question about its past effectiveness: If the pattern of land use is presently a problem, how will the extension of the zoning approach prove to be a solution to problems when it has been a cause of problems in the past?

Notes

1. See *Hadachek v. Los Angeles*, 239 U.S., 394.

2. See chapter 2, "An Economic Theory of Institutional Development," in G.C. Bjork, *Private Enterprise and Public Interest: The Development of American Capitalism* (Englewood Cliffs, N.J.: Prentice-Hall, 1969), pp. 20-34.

3. This is the distinction between the role of the state as *dominium* and *imperium*, discussed in chapter 4.

4. This section should not be construed as an argument for changing the level of revenues raised by taxes. This issue can be divorced from the question of incidence and structure.

5. For an elegant exposition of this argument, see Ronald Teeples, "A Model of a Matching Grant-in-Aid Program with External Tax Effects," *National Tax Journal* 22 (1969).

10 Prospects for Change

Approaching the control of land and the environment by shifting decisions to individual cost-benefit determinations is unlikely to excite much public enthusiasm. The environmental movement has come to see the preservation of the environment as a sacred trust rather than as a costly choice. The largely upper-middle-class adherents of environmental protection have been more interested in an "Onward Christian Soldiers" approach as they march off to war against the forces of evil than they have in examining who would bear the costs of their crusade.

Government agencies have been all too willing to increase their power over people and the control of the environment in the name of environmental protection. What bureaucrat, interested in extending his income and power, would not be in favor of comprehensive land-use planning and increased governmental control over private activities that use the environment?

Large individual and corporate landowners are unlikely to find the preceding proposals for changes in taxation and the assertion of public ownership of the environment as a basis for user charges attractive on grounds of economic self-interest. The proposals outlined would cost them money and lead in most cases to a decline in the value of their real estate assets, insofar as tax increases and user charges decrease the capitalized value of economic rents.

With all these interests arrayed against changes in the status quo, what are the practical possibilities of passage and implementation of the proposals outlined in the previous chapter? Perhaps, naïvely, I think they are better than might be assumed at first glance.

The assertion of public ownership of the environment as a basis for the imposition of use charges has the advantage over regulations or standards that it would produce some revenue. It also has the advantage of appealing to a firmly held American belief that those who enjoy the benefits of a particular economic activity should pay the costs. I find it very plausible that state legislatures would draft and pass legislation affirming state ownership of environmental quality as a basis for imposing user charges for its use.

I find it somewhat less likely that city or county governments would abandon zoning powers or that state legislatures would rescind the statutory powers for the exercise of zoning. It is not inconceivable, however, that the self-interests of property owners in more intensive development of their

129

properties than allowed by present zoning, coupled with the increase in tax revenues from the higher incomes derived from more intensively used real estate, might lead to increasing pressure for the relaxation of zoning requirements to allow more intensive use. The increasing use of "planned unit developments" in areas of new residential development is a harbinger of change in this area.

There is a natural coalition for the relaxation of zoning (accompanied by continuing standards for health and safety on a statewide level) between construction labor unions and the burgeoning population that wants lower prices for housing. The intensification of land use that could result from the abolition of zoning provisions that increase lot size and decrease housing density would allow for a reduction of land costs and an increase in construction activity and employment.

Changes in tax laws do not come easily. The political alliances that would be necessary to secure changes in federal tax law to end deductions for local property taxes from federal income-tax liability and the substitution of local, state, and federal income taxes based on income including the imputed value of land services is difficult to foresee.

Yet there are two factors that should not be overlooked as tax changes are contemplated. The first was the overwhelming passage of the Jarvis-Gann Amendment in California in 1978. While many factors contributed to the huge majority realized by this limitation of property taxes on real estate, one element in the election was a widespread feeling that property taxes were unfair. Implicitly at least, voters could be seen as opting for income taxes or sales taxes as a method of financing government.

The second factor that needs to be addressed is the whole question of federal revenue sharing with states and cities. There is increasing national pressure for a balanced federal budget even while state and local governments press the federal government for additional revenues. Congress could escape some of these pressures by ending federal revenue sharing and telling state and local governments to base their taxation on federal tax liability. It is hard to imagine this solution being sought by municipal or state officials or legislators, but it is not inconceivable that a national taxpayers' movement could push this reform as a way to limit the power of local governments by placing them in competition with one another and in full public view.

Requirements for public purchase of recreational areas and public planning in the siting of public facilities would be such obvious improvements in the conduct of government that it is difficult to see how these proposals could draw open criticism. Like the estimation of costs to be charged for the use of the environment, the requirement that public use of land be accompanied by economic- and environmental-impact statements should be welcomed by professional economists as much as zoning regulations and environmental legislation have been welcomed by the legal profession!

While public utilities and consumers' groups might have opposed the marginal-cost pricing of public utility services in the sixties for reasons suggested in the last chapter, the shortage of capital and the incredible increase in utility prices in the 1970s may very well have changed the balance of economic interests that would interact in state legislatures to consider such a proposal. Certainly, the increasing public recognition of limits to growth and concern for conservation of existing urban areas would make this proposal more politically feasible.[1]

The choices for Americans posed by more intensive utilization of land and resources will not become easier in the future, and they should not be made by government officials. The government has a substantial responsibility to create a social framework to allow those choices to be made by individual citizens with full knowledge of and responsibility for the costs. Choices about the use of resources are basically questions about individual values, and they need to be answered by individual rather than bureaucratic decisions.

Government officials have an important role to play in indicative planning. They should indicate the nature and costs of certain policy options, but the choices between those options need to be made by individuals through their legislative representatives with full knowledge of the trade-offs.

The political process cannot occur intelligently and responsibly unless the public is informed of the trade-offs. Our political rhetoric has too often concealed from us the hard reality that the pursuit of one goal makes us less able to realize others. This may be good short-run politics, but it has contributed to disillusionment with government by the American people when we are desperately in need of a strong social and political framework to assure sound choices about the wise use of scarce resources.

Those who expect more sweeping proposals for the protection of our environmental and political heritage than are encompassed in recommendations for changes in taxation, utility pricing, user fees, and zoning alterations may continue to search for comprehensive panaceas elsewhere than in the modification of property rights. They will not escape the necessity of making hard choices with real costs.

Note

1. A national public-opinion survey conducted in the mid-seventies identified two strong groups in conflict over land-use planning: environmentalists and localists. Careful examination of attitudes led to the conclusion that improvements in environmental controls were wanted by the public if protection from "faceless, incompetent, and arrogant state bureaucrats" could be assured. One survey conclusion was that a system for

control that assured "a high degree of public visibility and accountability" would make an altered framework for control of land and environment acceptable. See Steven R. Brown and James G. Coke, *Public Opinion on Land Use Regulation* (Columbus, Ohio: Academy for Contemporary Problems, 1977).

Index

Index

About the Author

Gordon C. Bjork is Jonathan B. Lovelace Professor of Economics at the Claremont Men's College and the Claremont Graduate School. He has held faculty appointments at the University of British Columbia, Carleton University, Oregon State University, and Columbia University. Dr. Bjork has served as a senior staff economist at the Batelle Institute and as president of Linfield College in Oregon. He was graduated from Dartmouth College, was a Rhodes Scholar at Oxford University, and received the Ph.D. in economics from the University of Washington.

Dr. Bjork has taught and published in a wide range of areas in economics. His last book, *Private Enterprise and Public Interest: The Development of American Capitalism*, was published in seven foreign languages. Dr. Bjork serves as a director or consultant for several corporations and is a frequent public speaker on various economic topics.